THE
DIVVIES BAKERY
COOKBOOK

THE
DIVVIES BAKERY
COOKBOOK

No Nuts. No Eggs. No Dairy.

Just Delicious!

LORI SANDLER

ST. MARTIN'S PRESS

NEW YORK

This book is intended as a reference, not as a medical manual. The information given here is not intended
as a substitute for any dietary regimen that may have been prescribed by your doctor. Neither the publisher
nor the author accept any legal responsibility for any personal injury or damages arising from the use or misuse
of the information and advice in this book.

THE DIVVIES BAKERY COOKBOOK. Copyright © 2010 by Lori Sandler. All rights reserved.
Printed in China. For information address St. Martin's Press, 175 Fifth Avenue, New York, N.Y. 10010.

Cover design by Lisa Pompilio
Interior illustrations by Kim Ronemus, Richard Testani, Tom Lewek, Kim Ronemus Design
Photography by Thomas Dilworth, Aristo Studios
Prop and set styling by Tamara Dilworth
Food styling by Justine Poldino
Book design by Maggie Hoffman

ISBN 978-0-312-60528-5

First Edition: August 2010

10 9 8 7 6 5 4 3 2 1

With all the love in my heart,

I dedicate this book to Mark, Adam, Max, and Benjamin.

made to share

· ·

Divvies believes eating and celebrating should

always be a shared, inclusive experience,

not exclusive to those without food allergies.

CONTENTS

It's Your Party! 113

MAKE YOUR OWN PARTY FAVORS 136

THE
DIVVIES BAKERY
COOKBOOK

Introduction

If you were a kid during the 1970s, you may remember a Dr. Seuss book called *My Book About Me*. It required the owner (me) to fill in the blanks with such important personal information as "I have _____ freckles on my face." If you'd like to know, I had exactly twenty-two freckles, which I was certain of because I put a little pen mark on each one in order not to double count. When I came to the part about "What I want to be when I grow up," I first wrote "teacher," then crossed it out and rewrote "bakery lady." At seven years old, there was nothing quite like going to a bakery and being offered a little butter cookie by the bakery lady. I have no idea if she was the same lady each time I went, I just knew that I loved being offered, accepting, and enjoying that cookie.

I am not your typical bakery lady. I didn't go to culinary school. I majored in business. The inspiration who resparked my early desire to become a bakery lady is our youngest son, Benjamin.

Because Benjamin was born with many food allergies, he could not enjoy the same bakery experience I had as a child. The butter and eggs in the delicious cookies I enjoyed would be life-threatening. There was Benjamin, living life to the fullest, "not letting food allergies define him," as he now says—yet he really was excluded when it came to eating treats. Becoming a bakery lady has evolved as a result of my labor of love—Divvies Bakery—a dedicated peanut-free, tree nut–free, milk-free, and egg-free facility (parts are gluten-free, too), located in beautiful South Salem, New York.

So, how did I come up with the idea for Divvies? When Benjamin was just born, he had some of the telltale signs of food allergies. We carefully monitored everything we ate and touched when we were near him in order to prevent any form of an allergic reaction. A wise industrial designer once said, "It isn't that a person is handicapped because he only has one leg, it's just that we've designed his world for people with two legs." Same goes with food allergies. We don't need our world to be turned upside down because of these allergies; instead, we have to design the right food. I've been doing just that since the time it became clear that Benjamin had severe food allergies, and that we would need to strike eggs, nuts, and milk from his diet.

I envisioned preparing meals for my family that avoided these ingredients, but when it came to food kids loved the most—sweets—I couldn't imagine how we'd make it work. Benjamin's first birthday "cake" was a stroke of sheer genius: a candle on top of a glistening tower of shaved ice. While Benjamin was completely enthralled with this frozen creation (and didn't even give the decadent chocolate cake that the rest of us were eating a passing glance), I knew it would meet with the same fate as Frosty, and its appeal would melt away as Benjamin got older. Birthday celebrations two and three yielded products that were more cakelike in appearance, but nothing anyone other than Benjamin and a few adventurous friends cared to coax down their throats. As diligently as I experimented with various egg and butter substitutes, the texture and the taste of these confections were similar to rubber. I had to act fast. As Benjamin grew, so did his friends and their awareness that he was definitely not eating what they were eating.

My big push to literally turn the (designated lunch) tables on food allergies came when Benjamin voiced his dismay at being labeled the "kid with food allergies." That was my call to action to create the most scrumptious sweets his friends had ever tasted, all made without nuts, eggs, and milk. What followed were many years of testing, tasting, redoes, and refining; of listening to Benjamin, his brothers, Adam and Max, and their friends; and of thinking outside the traditional bakery box and finally coming up with a lot of wildly kid-popular recipes. What I didn't realize I was also developing along the way were great shortcuts (to get me out of the kitchen and back with the family); last-minute tricks (so I don't "freak out" when I am told Sunday night there is a class party on Monday); must-haves for the pantry (to whip up after-school snacks if everyone ends up at our home); food that can travel (so when the flight is cancelled, we are prepared); and useful advice for communicating with teachers and parents (so no one feels put out or put upon to make everyone feel included). The other thing I learned is that two ingredients are common in all of those recipes: a pound of patience and a heaping helping of humor.

So, Benjamin finally became the kid with the "goods." He was the go-to person to share lunch bag treats; to bring desserts for class parties; to supply snacks for after school. But that wasn't enough for me, or for my husband, Mark. We wanted to make sure that every child with food allergies to nuts, eggs, and milk could walk into their classroom with delicious treats to share. And that vision is what led us to start a sweet-treat company with a dedicated no-nut, no-egg, no-milk bakery and call it Divvies. The very name connotes "divvying up" treats—a one-for-me-and-one-for-you equation.

In the spirit of Divvies, I have written a book filled with recipes for delicious, safe treats that everyone will want to share, with or without food allergies, as well as tips, hints, shortcuts, and "life recipes" that will help everyone feel included. The treats are divided into sections that focus on the times in our lives when food plays an important role; times when there is a potential for those who can't eat certain foods to feel very left out. So the recipes are actually sweet antidotes to each of these events: family celebrations, school parties, travel, and birthdays. I've even included a section called "Snack Attack," which is filled with fun and delicious snacks that take less than ten minutes to make.

Life's little pleasure of delicious desserts is now *made to share,* so dig in and welcome to the world of DIVVIES!

A sweet story about Divvies Bakery...

We received a call from a mom who asked if she and her family could bring their little girl, who has severe food allergies, to visit Divvies Bakery. They explained that she always felt excluded at parties and gatherings because she couldn't enjoy the same sweet treats as her family and friends. We gladly invited her, and she packed up the whole family (Grandma and Grandpa included), and traveled four hours to visit us at the bakery. When they arrived, my husband, Mark, greeted everyone and then got down to eye-level with the little girl and told her that she was to be his guest at the bakery and that only she would be allowed inside. It was a magical, *Charlie and the Chocolate Factory*–like moment. "This is the land of yes," he told her, "and everything that we are making inside is safe and delicious for you to eat." He put a hairnet on her head, as if crowning her the "chosen one" to enter through the Divvies doors, took her hand, and led her into our bakery, stacked high with popcorn, cookies, candy, cupcakes, and chocolate. Her family watched the little tour through the bakery window with tears streaming down their faces. The sight of this child walking awestruck among treats that had been off limits her whole life was an emotional and joyful experience for everyone—Mark and me included.

A Note from Benjamin

If I could have one wish come true, it would be to outgrow my food allergies. I have had food allergies for my whole life. It hasn't always been easy, because I always have to check all the labels of foods. Whenever I go to a restaurant, I have to ask about all the ingredients and make sure my meal is made safely. If I did eat something I am allergic to, my throat would close up, and I would have to go to the emergency room. As you can see, my food allergies would be a good thing to get rid of.

When I was little, I thought it wasn't fair that I had food allergies, and when it came to eating, I didn't like being at birthday parties. Since I have gotten older, I can handle attending birthday parties without my parents, and communicating about my food allergies and what needs to be done with food in order for me to be safe.

I still get frustrated when everyone can eat something I can't have. But I just take a deep breath and break out food my mom has sent along with me to the party that I know everyone will enjoy.

Bringing something that everyone likes to eat and everyone can share—that makes me feel great!

Benjamin's Top 10

You should try some of these recipes. Most are pretty easy to make. Not that I know for sure (I usually just stir the batter and eat the final product), but I have definitely tasted enough to let you know which are my personal favorites:

Robin's Apple Pie

Cinnamon Buns

Gingersnaps

Oh Fudge!

Grape Soda

Root Beer Floats

Divvies Famous Chocolate Cupcakes

Blondies

Cookie S'Mores

Chocolate Chip Cookie Dough Ice Cream

Before You Begin

Be sure to read and reread ingredient labels every time you shop in case manufacturers change their recipes, ingredients, or production procedures. This may lead to an introduction of allergens in products that used to be considered safe.

Read Labels Carefully

Teach your children (with and without food allergies), friends, family, coaches, camp counselors, and teachers how to read labels. It is absolutely essential that they know what to look for and what to question. When in doubt, don't use an ingredient until you are absolutely certain it is safe. Believe it or not, this often means calling the manufacturer directly. The good news is that labeling laws have become more stringent over the years, and are always improving.

Divvies is grateful for all the wonderful work the Food Allergy Initiative (www.faiusa.org) and the Food Allergy and Anaphylaxis Network (www.foodallergy.org) are doing to help people living with food allergies, their families, and communities. I highly recommend you visit their websites to learn more about their fine work and goals. Both sites provide a wealth of information about food allergies and their progressive research to find a cure for food allergies.

Cross-contamination

According to the Food Allergy Initiative, the only way to avoid an allergic reaction is to strictly avoid the allergy-inducing food. This is why it's essential to be diligent about avoiding cross-contamination. Cross-contamination occurs when one food comes into contact with another food and their proteins mix. As a result, each food then contains small amounts of the other food, often invisible to us. Such contact may be either direct (e.g., placing cheese on a hamburger) or indirect via hands or utensils. The protein is the component of the food that causes the food allergy. A tiny amount of an allergenic food is enough to cause an allergic reaction in some people. Therefore, precautions must be taken to avoid cross-contact with foods a person is allergic to.

In addition to always having baking basics such as flour, sugar, and vanilla on hand, you'll want to be sure to stock your kitchen with the following items, most of which are easy to find in many grocery stores:

In the Pantry

- Divvies® Semisweet Chocolate Chips are the best tasting safe chocolate chips, if I do say so myself. They take 2 minutes to melt in a microwave (and everything tastes better when dipped in chocolate!).
- PAM Baking no-stick baking spray contains flour and makes preparing pans before baking a simple task.
- PAM Original no-stick cooking spray is fantastic for coating spoons, saucepans,

and mixing bowls so ingredients like melted marshmallows and honey will slide right off.

- Marshmallows—use Dandies from Chicago Soy Dairy if you prefer vegan marshmallows made in a nut-free facility.
- Gummy Candy—use Surf Sweets, available for purchase at www.surfsweets .com and on www.Amazon.com if you prefer vegan gummies. Surf Sweets makes nut-free, vegan fruity bears, gummy swirls, and sour worms.
- Ener-G Egg Replacer is a miracle worker for binding cookies and cakes just as well as eggs.
- Plain Seltzer makes cakes light and airy.
- White Vinegar is the coolest egg substitute ever.
- Canola Oil is a great egg substitute that doesn't change the taste of baked goods.
- Spectrum Organic Trans-fat-free Shortening works well for those who prefer baked goods made with shortening in place of butter or margarine. Please read more about "dairy-free butter substitutes" in Divvies Baking Basics on page 14.
- Applesauce makes your desserts sweeter and moister.
- Corn Syrup, when used sparingly in brownies and toppings, adds just the right amount of sweetness.
- Divvies® Frosting is so creamy and delicious; keep it on hand for when you don't feel like making frosting from scratch.
- Confectioners' Sugar gives that extra-yummy and decorative touch.
- Nut-, Dairy-, and Egg-free Candies, especially Divvies Jelly Beans, Rock Candy, and Super Stars, are great for decorating desserts and food projects.
- Divvies® Popcorn Kernels pop up huge! Use them for the best movie snack ever.

- Licorice "Straws"—while everyone else holds their drinks with their pinkies in the air, you'll be blowing bubbles through your licorice straw!
- To make everything taste yummier and look more festive have on hand a good supply of sprinkles, crushed peppermint, non-pareils, etc.

In the Refrigerator

- Silk Soy Milk and/or Rice Dream Rice Milk are great substitutes for milk.
- Silk Creamer makes very creamy fudge. This ingredient is not sold in all grocery stores, so you may want to call and ask for it.
- Nasoya Silken Tofu is another great egg substitute. Puree the contents of the entire box, and store in an airtight container in the refrigerator. Be sure to strain excess water before using in recipes.
- Tofutti Milk-free Better Than Sour Cream is the secret ingredient (now out-of-the-bag) in my brownies.
- Tofutti Milk-free Better Than Cream Cheese makes delicious cream cheese frosting.
- Earth Balance Vegan Buttery Sticks is a great butter substitute for mixing into fruit fillings for pies. Please read more about "dairy-free butter substitutes" in Divvies Baking Basics on page 14.
- Fleischmann's Unsalted Margarine is a great butter substitute for cookies, cakes, frostings, and bars.
- Earth Balance Natural Shortening works nicely for those who prefer baked goods made with shortening in place of butter or margarine.

In the Freezer

- Tofutti Nondairy and Organic SO Delicious Dairy-free Frozen Desserts are Benjamin's favorite ice cream substitutes. The rest of our family loves them, too!

- Sorbet—we always keep raspberry-flavored sorbet ready to be scooped into our "Brown" Chocolate Bags!

Equipment

- Parchment paper
- 9 × 9-inch and 8 × 8-inch pans, and 12 × 8-inch pans, or close to it; you don't need to be exact!
- Two to three edged cookie sheets for when you're baking for a crowd
- Two cupcake pans that make 1 dozen cupcakes each
- Two 9-inch glass pie plates (standard size)
- Bundt pan
- Aluminum loaf pans, mini (5 × 3-inch) and medium (9 × 5-inch)
- Four 5½-inch pie plates for IPies (see page 96)
- Rubber spatulas—you can never scrape the sides of a mixing bowl enough!
- Mini stainless steel icing spatula for frosting cupcakes, icing cakes, spreading chocolate over frozen bananas, and filling in the corners of chocolate bags
- Mixing bowls from 2- to 8-quart capacity
- Mini bowl that holds 1 to 2 cups
- 8-inch whisk
- 8-inch stainless steel strainer for sifting dry ingredients
- Measuring spoons
- Measuring cups
- #24, #30, and #40-size ice-cream scoops for scooping cookie dough, sorbet, and nondairy "ice cream"
- 1-, 2-, and 3-quart saucepans
- Wire cooling rack
- Paper bowls to make cleanup of melted chocolate much easier

- Standard-size and mini-size paper cupcake liners, for chocolate-dipped delicacies, cupcakes, and muffins
- 10-inch wooden skewers for candy and fruit shish kabobs
- Festive trays for adding extra wow to your desserts
- Doilies—a little sophistication never hurt anybody
- Popsicle and lollipop sticks for Chocolate-Covered Monkey Pops and Chocolate-Covered Marshmallows
- Unused coffee bean bags for making "Brown" Chocolate Bags (page 42)
- Electric stand mixer or hand mixer
- Chocolate Fountain, which can be found at a reasonable price at many large discount retail stores
- Food processor
- Candy thermometer

Divvies Baking Basics

Preparing to Bake

- Clean hands are an absolute must!
- Be sure to clear and clean all work surfaces.
- Check that all pans, mixing blades, and other utensils are clean and do not have any residue from previously baked items. Since I never bake with nuts, milk, or eggs, our appliances and utensils are free of even trace amounts of these allergens. You may want to either dedicate specific cooking tools for allergen-free baking and cooking, or choose to be extra-vigilant when it comes to cleanup.
- It's nice to have a fresh holding bin for used dishes, so make sure you start with a clean and empty sink. It helps make the whole baking process simple and less confusing, and makes cleanup a cinch.

- Have an empty trash container nearby (or at least one that isn't completely full!)—once again, keep things neat and simple.
- Have all cleaning tools in close reach, including liquid soap, sponges, dish towels, and paper goods. Be vigilant about ensuring your sponge is free of allergens!
- If your kids are helping you bake, and something spills on the floor, clean it up right away, so nobody slips.

Read and Assemble

Before starting any recipe, read through the instructions. Then assemble all ingredients, utensils, and equipment to make certain you have everything on hand.

Always Read and Reread Ingredient Labels

I can't stress this enough. Even if you are purchasing the same product for the hundredth time, reread the label to make sure it is free of allergens and possible cross-contamination. Most manufacturers are well prepared to answer your questions about how their products are produced, so don't hesitate to call or e-mail them.

Follow Recipes in Ingredient Order

Recipes will be easier to make if you follow each step in the order it has been written.

Measure All Ingredients Accurately

Baking really is a science. Take care in precisely measuring all ingredients.

Scrape that Mixing Bowl!

Scraping down the sides of the mixing bowl during the mixing process ensures that all the ingredients will be fully incorporated.

Let's Talk About Substituting Butter

Creating delicious recipes for desserts that everyone will love *without butter* can be a challenge. Whenever I read recipes that call for "dairy-free spreads" or "butter substitutes," I usually try making them with Fleischmann's Unsalted Margarine first. I've read so many different opinions about various substitutions. I hope the following guidelines will help you select products you are most comfortable using.

- Dairy-free Butter Substitutes, Dairy-free Margarines, Shortenings: While butter and Fleischmann's Unsalted Margarine have some water in them, shortening does not, producing a different texture. Take cookies, for example: Cookies made with shortening and no extra water added are higher and lighter, while those made with margarine are flatter and a bit crispier. This is because margarine has a lower melting point than shortening, causing cookies to spread faster during baking. Not all brands are dairy-free! That's why you must always be vigilant about reading labels.
- Dairy-free Margarine Options for Cakes, Cookies, Loaves, Cupcakes, Bars, and Brownies: Try Fleischmann's Unsalted Margarine (www.fleischmanns.com), Earth Balance Natural Shortening (www.EarthBalanceNatural.com), Earth Balance Vegan Buttery Sticks, and Spectrum Organic Trans-fat Free Shortening (www.spectrumorganics.com)
- All-Vegetable Shortening: If you use shortening and want the results to be similar to using Fleishmann's Unsalted Margarine, add 2 tablespoons of

water for every 1 cup of shortening, or reduce the amount of shortening to ¾ cup for every 1 cup of dairy-free margarine.

• Dairy-free Margarine Options for Frostings and Fruit Fillings for Pies: **Try Earth Balance Vegan Buttery Sticks or Fleischmann's Unsalted Margarine.**

Preparing Ener-G Egg Replacer

Whisking powdered egg replacer and water together ensures that it will fully dissolve. Once dissolved, use a spatula to remove every last drop from the prep bowl to incorporate with the other ingredients.

Pureeing Silken Tofu

When using tofu as an egg substitute in recipes, it's best to puree it before measuring so that pieces of tofu do not appear in your baked goods. If you choose to keep a supply of pureed tofu in the refrigerator, water will separate from the tofu during storage. Each time you use it, simply place the tofu in a colander to drain the water before measuring.

Write in this Book!

Make notes in the margins to remind yourself who loved which recipes, tricks you discovered that made a step easier, ingredient brands you prefer to use, etc. For example, perhaps you like the way a recipe turns out using one flavor of fruit preserves better than another—record it while you're making the recipe, so you don't forget! I've also included a few pages in the back of the book for your notes, so jot away!

Pretend You Are the Star of Your Own Cooking Show!

- Before starting a recipe, read through it carefully from start to finish to ensure that you understand all of the steps involved.

- On days that I have the time to be extra organized, I prep and measure all of my ingredients into individual bowls before baking—very much like you see chefs do on a cooking show! Preparing the *mise en place* ahead of time allows you to bake without having to stop and assemble items.

- Often, if I know I will be making several batches of the same recipe over the course of a few days, I will premeasure, mix, and store prepared, dry ingredients in individual containers.

- Keep multiple sets of measuring spoons and cups on hand for quick ingredient prep.

- Don an apron; kids love wearing aprons and chef's hats, and it makes for a cute photo op.

- Have dish towels and oven mitts on hand.

- When you are finished baking, put all of your ingredients back in their original storage spaces so you will be able to find them easily the next time.

WHEN IT'S ALL RELATIVE(S)— AND FRIENDS

Treats that Sweeten the Familial Pot

Celebrations and Holidays

Holidays bring the family together. All those relatives bearing tins and platters of cherished family recipes, as intricately woven into the fabric of their being as Grandma's embroidered tablecloths. Worried about having to ask everyone to check their goods at the door? You don't have to be! You just need to engage in a little family "counseling" prior to the get-together. In your world, what they may not know *can* hurt the person with food allergies, so you need to educate and provide sweet solutions.

Whether or not your family members are able to bring allergen-free desserts to your gatherings, you'll want to whip up the recipes in this section. These are the decadent superstars of desserts; the all-out crowd-pleasers that will keep everyone at the gathering sweetly in the mix.

When planning a celebration at your own home

- Remember that inclusivity should be your highest priority.
- Try to make as many dishes as possible be safe for everyone.
- Bundle up extra portions of the delicious allergen-safe desserts so your guests may take them home and remember just how good "made without" can taste.
- Save the packaging from all the ingredients in your dishes just in case a guest with food allergies has a question about them.
- Keep your sense of humor—remember, this is a celebration!

When you are going to someone else's home to celebrate

- Don't assume they remember anyone's food allergies.
- Call ahead and suggest foods your host can make that are super-easy and allergen-free.
- Offer to make and bring a variety of desserts that are made to share.

Warm Apple-Apricot Cake

This is one of my favorite cake recipes, since it's just as delicious and moist as the traditional, butter-laden version. For a super-moist cake, add 4 cups of apples and 1 cup of apricot fruit spread. I like to serve this cake warm out of the oven for brunch but it's delicious served at room temperature, too.

1. Preheat the oven to 350 degrees.
2. Spray a bundt-style pan with nonstick baking spray.
3. Whisk together the flour, salt, cinnamon, baking soda, and baking powder in a bowl and set aside.
4. In a separate bowl, whip together the oil and sugar with an electric mixer, increasing gradually to high speed, for a total of 3 minutes. Add the applesauce and apricot and mix on high speed for another minute until creamy.
5. Add the dry ingredients to the wet and mix on medium speed until well incorporated. Scrape down the sides of the bowl with a spatula and continue mixing. The batter will clump together.
6. Add the apples to the batter and mix on low speed until well combined. Pour the batter (which will be very thick) into the prepared pan.
7. Bake in the oven for 60 to 70 minutes, rotating the pan halfway through baking. Test the center of the cake for doneness with a toothpick. The cake may take a bit longer to bake if the apples are particularly juicy, because the center will be extra moist. Turn the cake out of the pan onto a cooling rack immediately after removing from the oven.

Makes 1 bundt cake; 12 slices

3 cups flour

1 teaspoon salt

3/4 teaspoon ground cinnamon

1 teaspoon baking soda

1 teaspoon baking powder

1½ cups canola oil

1½ cups sugar

½ cup applesauce

1/3 cup apricot all-fruit spread (apricot jam)

3 cups ¼-inch-thick diced pieces of peeled, cored Granny Smith apples (about 5 apples)

One kid's 4-ounce snack pack–size of applesauce = just about ½ cup applesauce

Banana Bread (or Muffins!)

Here's my delicious take on a time-honored favorite. These are easy to bake ahead of time and keep in the freezer, so you have them on hand when out-of-town guests stay over for breakfast. You can also add chocolate chips and voila—you've got a great dessert muffin.

3½ cups all-purpose flour

2 teaspoons baking soda

1½ teaspoons salt

1 teaspoon ground cinnamon

1 teaspoon ground nutmeg

½ teaspoon ground cloves

½ teaspoon ground ginger

5 very ripe, peeled bananas (no rotten bananas!)

1 cup applesauce

1 cup canola oil

½ cup water

3 cups granulated sugar

½ cup packed dark brown sugar for sprinkling on top of loaf (optional)

1. Preheat the oven to 375 degrees. Spray either three 9 × 5-inch loaf pans, six 5 × 3-inch mini loaf pans, or a muffin pan (depending on desired size and quantity) with nonstick baking spray. If you line the muffin pan with paper liners, you do not need to spray the pan. For variety, mix it up! Try baking one loaf, two mini loaves, and six or more muffins.

2. Whisk together the flour, baking soda, salt, cinnamon, nutmeg, cloves, and ginger in a medium bowl. Set aside.

3. Peel the bananas and add them to a separate mixing bowl. Beat with an electric mixer on medium speed until pureed. Add the applesauce, canola oil, water, and sugar. Continue beating until the sugar has dissolved and all the ingredients are well combined.

4. Add the flour mixture to the wet ingredients. Beat on medium speed. Be sure to thoroughly scrape down the sides of the bowl and the mixing paddle in order to incorporate all the ingredients. Continue beating for another minute. If there are still lumps of dry flour in the batter, scrape down the sides of the bowl and mix one more time.

5. Add 1 cup of the desired mix-in, and pour the batter into the prepared pans.

6. If desired, lightly sprinkle a thin layer of brown

sugar on top of the muffins before placing them in the oven. For loaves, sprinkle the brown sugar on top after they have been baking for at least 10 minutes.

7. Full-size loaves may take up to 80 minutes to bake through (check for doneness at 65 minutes). Mini loaves take 45 to 60 minutes, and muffins 25 to 27 minutes. Baking time may be a bit longer if you've added fruit as your mix-in. Test for doneness by inserting a toothpick or sharp knife into the center of the loaf or muffin. If it comes out clean, the loaf or muffins are ready to come out of the oven.

8. Remove from oven and place the pans on wire racks. Let muffins cool for 10 minutes and loaves for 20 minutes; they will continue to bake a bit during this time. Then remove from the pan so they do not overbake.

Makes three 9 × 5-inch loaves or six 5 × 3-inch mini loaves or 12 muffins

I love asking my kids what type of muffins they prefer and then customizing the batch to suit their individual tastes. It's easier than it sounds and makes the boys so happy (not as happy as a snow day off from school, of course!). Simply pour plain batter into each muffin cup, then place 7 chocolate chips or 7 blueberries, etc. on top. Use a small spoon to distribute the fruit or chips throughout the batter.

Every fall while growing up in Maine, my friend Robin would go to the apple orchard for apples with her mother, who would make several of these pies. Robin always helped out in the kitchen and made mini pies for herself! She has continued the tradition in her own family and makes pies every fall for her children after going to the orchard. This is Benjamin's favorite apple pie. Note that Robin uses all organic ingredients except for the shortening.

2 cups sifted flour

1 cup Crisco All-Vegetable Shortening

½ teaspoon salt

3 to 4 tablespoons cold water

¾ cup sugar

1 teaspoon ground cinnamon

6 to 7 apples, Cortland, McIntosh, Granny Smith, or a mixture; if apples are very large you may use only 5

½ teaspoon lemon juice

1 tablespoon sugar for sprinkling on top of the pie

For the Pie Crust

1. Preheat the oven to 425 degrees.

2. Mix together the flour and salt in a large bowl.

3. Add the shortening to the flour and salt mixture using a rubber spatula. Cut the shortening into the flour mixture. The pieces of shortening should be about the size of peas.

4. Slowly add the water tablespoon by tablespoon and mix lightly with a fork until all the flour is moistened into a ball.

5. Continue to shape the mixture into a ball with your hands and wrap in wax paper or plastic wrap. Refrigerate overnight, or from morning to evening.

6. Spray two 9-inch pie plates or four 5½-inch mini pie dishes with nonstick baking spray made with flour.

7. Remove the dough from the refrigerator and remold into a ball. Cut the ball in half and roll each half into a smaller ball.

8. Take two sheets of wax paper and sprinkle and spread flour over one piece.

9. Place one dough ball on the floured sheet of wax paper and sprinkle a little flour on top of dough.

10. Put the second sheet of wax paper on top and then

roll the dough out with a rolling pin, until very thin and large enough in diameter to fit your pie pan.

11. Remove the top sheet of wax paper, flip the dough over, and then press it into the pie dish. Gently peel off the top piece of wax paper.

12. Sprinkle a little flour on the bottom of the pie shell, which will help to absorb some of the liquid from the apples.

For the Filling

1. Mix the sugar and cinnamon together in a small bowl.

2. Wash the apples thoroughly, peel, and slice thinly.

3. Dry the apple slices with paper towels to remove excess water, and place in a large bowl.

4. Pour the sugar and cinnamon mixture over the apples, pour the lemon juice on top, and toss to mix.

5. Pour the apple mixture into the pie shell.

6. Roll out the other half of the pie dough, following the directions above, and place carefully on top of the apple mixture. Peel off the wax paper.

7. Use the tines of a fork to make eight to ten fork holes on top of each pie, or make three slits with a sharp knife across the top crust before baking. Use the fork (or your fingers) to press the edges of the two layers of dough together all around the pie dish.

8. Sprinkle sugar on top of the pie.

9. Bake in the preheated oven for 45 to 50 minutes, or until golden brown.

Makes two 9-inch pies or 4 mini IPies

> If you plan to freeze the pie rather than serve it immediately, bake it for 35 to 40 minutes, allow to cool completely, and then wrap well with aluminum foil. The pies will freeze well for at least 6 months.

Cinnamon Buns

These are so delicious hot out of the oven as well as the next day! The gooey cinnamon and sugar filling keeps these buns nice and moist. While the icing is delicious, we enjoy ours without! For an extra-special breakfast treat, prepare the dough the night before and bake them in the morning.

THE DOUGH

¼ cup silken tofu

2 cups soy milk or rice milk, at room temperature

⅔ cup dairy-free margarine, melted

4½ cups unbleached flour

1 teaspoon salt

½ cup sugar

2½ teaspoons active dry yeast

THE FILLING

1 cup packed brown sugar

¼ cup granulated sugar

1½ tablespoons ground cinnamon

6 tablespoons dairy-free margarine, softened

½ cup raisins (optional)

1. Place the silken tofu in the food processor and pulse until completely pureed.

2. Mix all dough ingredients on high speed for 2 to 3 minutes, or until well combined. Be sure to scrape down the sides of bowl to thoroughly incorporate all the ingredients. Cover with a dish towel or plastic wrap and set aside in a warm place for 30 minutes, or until almost doubled.

3. Spray a 13 × 9-inch baking pan with nonstick baking spray.

4. Pour the sugars and cinnamon into a small bowl and mix with a spoon until well combined. Set aside.

5. Lay out two sheets of wax paper, each at least 24 inches in length. Lightly spray each with nonstick baking spray. Turn the dough out onto the wax paper and place second sheet of wax paper on top, so that the dough is sandwiched between the two sprayed sides.

6. Roll the dough into a rectangle approximately 24 × 14 inches. Spread the dough with margarine and sprinkle evenly with the sugar/cinnamon mixture and the raisins, if using.

7. Beginning with a short side, carefully and firmly roll up the dough like a jelly roll. Using a very sharp

knife, slice into twelve equal-size rolls. Place the rolls on the prepared baking pan sliced sides up. Cover the unbaked cinnamon buns with a dish cloth, and let rise for another 30 minutes. At this point, preheat the oven to 400 degrees.

8. Bake the rolls in the preheated oven for 20 to 25 minutes. Test with a toothpick to make sure dough in the center of each bun is baked through.

For the Icing

1. While the rolls are baking, prepare the icing by beating together the "cream cheese," margarine, confectioners' sugar, vanilla, and salt. Scrape down the sides of the mixing bowl with a spatula and continue to beat until smooth. Spread the desired amount of frosting on the warm rolls before removing them from the pan to serve.

Makes 1 dozen 4-inch buns

THE "CREAM CHEESE" ICING (OPTIONAL)

1/2 cup Tofutti Better Than Cream Cheese

1/4 cup dairy-free margarine, softened

1 1/2 cups confectioners' sugar

1 teaspoon vanilla extract

1/8 teaspoon salt

Blueberry Cake

This is such a favorite among our boys and their friends that I just go ahead and precut the whole cake into squares—and watch it disappear. Plus, your guests will be amazed that this recipe is completely free of butter!

2½ cups cake flour

2½ teaspoons baking powder

½ teaspoon salt

1½ teaspoons powdered egg replacer

2 tablespoons seltzer

½ cup dairy-free margarine

1 cup plus ¼ cup sugar

1½ teaspoons vanilla extract

½ cup plus 2 tablespoons soy milk

2 cups blueberries, stems removed, washed, and dry

½ tablespoon ground cinnamon

1. Preheat the oven to 350 degrees. Spray a 9 × 9-inch or 12 × 8-inch pan with nonstick baking spray.
2. Whisk together the cake flour, baking powder, and salt and set aside.
3. Whisk the egg replacer and seltzer in a small bowl until well dissolved and frothy. Set aside.
4. Cream the margarine thoroughly with an electric mixer on high speed. Gradually add the 1 cup of sugar and cream well, scraping down the sides of the bowl with a spatula.
5. Add the egg replacer mixture and vanilla and beat thoroughly. Once again, be sure to scrape down the sides of the bowl as you mix.
6. Add the flour alternately with the soy milk, one-third at a time, beating well after each addition and until the batter is smooth; the batter will be stiff.
7. Fold the blueberries gently into the batter with a spoon and disperse evenly.
8. Spread the batter evenly into the prepared pan.
9. In a small bowl, mix the remaining ¼ cup sugar and cinnamon. Then sprinkle the mixture generously over the entire top of the cake batter.
10. Bake the cake in the preheated oven for 45 minutes,

rotating the pan 180 degrees halfway through the baking time. After 45 minutes, check the center for doneness with a toothpick. The cake can be served straight from the pan.

Makes one 9 × 9-inch cake; 12 squares or one 12 × 8-inch cake; 16 squares

Transform Your Picky Eater

Kids can be very picky eaters, whether or not they have food allergies. I have found that by including my kids in the fun of cooking (and especially baking!), they become much more adventurous about what they'll eat—mostly because they've had a hand in making it. I find this especially true with Benjamin, who knows that food is a black-and-white issue for him; it's either safe or it's not. When he helps me in our kitchen, where he knows everything is safe, Benjamin realizes how much he actually *can* eat and becomes engaged in the process, and proud of the delicious results that can be shared with the family.

Blueberry-Plum Upside-Down Cake

This cake makes for an impressive presentation. Have fun creating designs with various fruits and berries such as pineapples and raspberries.

THE TOPPING

½ cup dairy-free margarine

½ cup packed dark brown sugar

3 to 4 plums, pitted, cut into ½-inch wedges (peaches and pineapples work, too)

1½ pints blueberries (raspberries are great, too)

THE CAKE

1½ cups all-purpose flour

2 teaspoons baking powder

¾ teaspoon ground cinnamon

¼ teaspoon salt

3 teaspoons powdered egg replacer

4 tablespoons seltzer

¼ cup dairy-free margarine, at room temperature

1 cup sugar

1 teaspoon vanilla extract

1½ cups plus 1 tablespoon soy milk

1. Preheat the oven to 350 degrees. Use a 9-inch diameter round cake pan with 2-inch sides. Spray the sides of the pan with nonstick baking spray made with flour.

2. Melt the margarine in a saucepan over low heat. Add sugar and whisk until dissolved and the mixture forms a syrup.

3. Pour the syrup into the prepared pan and spread to cover the bottom.

4. Press the plums into the syrup in a circular pattern around the edge of the pan. Spread the blueberries in the center. If using other fruit, such as pineapples and/or berries, be sure to cover the entire bottom of the pan (for example, put raspberries inside pineapple rings). (This step may be done up to 2 hours prior to making the cake.) Let stand at room temperature.

5. Whisk the flour, baking powder, cinnamon, and salt in a bowl and set aside.

6. Whisk the powdered egg replacer with the seltzer in a small bowl until well dissolved and frothy. Set aside.

7. Beat the margarine with an electric mixer on high speed until smooth. Gradually add the sugar and continue beating on high speed. Be sure to scrape down the sides of the bowl with a spatula, and continue beating until everything is well incorporated.

8. Add the egg replacer and vanilla. Beat well, scraping down the sides of the bowl.

9. Beat the dry ingredients and soy milk alternately into the wet ingredients, again scraping down the sides of the bowl.

10. Spoon the batter over the topping.

11. Bake in the preheated oven for 40 minutes until the cake is golden and firm. To test for doneness, insert a toothpick into the cake layer only. When it comes out clean, the cake is done.

12. Remove the cake from the oven and let cool for 10 minutes on a wire rack. Run a knife around the edges. Place an inverted plate over the pan. Flip over the plate and cake to release the cake onto the plate. If the cake doesn't slip out of the pan, let it stand for 3 more minutes. Carefully remove the pan from the cake. Serve warm or at room temperature.

Makes one 9-inch round cake; 10 slices

To avoid a mess, place a sheet of aluminum foil on the oven rack just under the cake pan in case fruit syrup spills over.

Extra-Luscious Lemon Loaf

This cake is so moist and has just the right amount of tartness. I suggest you double the recipe and make two loaves since this disappears faster than you can imagine!

THE LEMON LOAF

1½ cups unbleached flour

1 teaspoon baking powder

⅛ teaspoon baking soda

½ teaspoon salt

1¼ cups granulated sugar

½ cup silken tofu, pureed

¼ cup applesauce

1 tablespoon white vinegar

⅛ cup grated lemon zest (about 3 lemons)

⅛ cup fresh lemon juice

1 cup dairy-free margarine, melted and cooled to room temperature

¼ cup dairy-free sour cream

1 teaspoon vanilla extract

THE LEMON SYRUP

¼ cup freshly squeezed lemon juice

¼ cup granulated sugar

For the Lemon Loaf

1. Preheat the oven to 350 degrees. Spray a 9 × 5-inch loaf pan with nonstick cooking spray. Line just the bottom of the pan with parchment paper, then spray the paper as well.

2. Sift the flour, baking powder, baking soda, and salt into a large bowl and set aside.

3. In a food processor, pulse the sugar, silken tofu, applesauce, vinegar, lemon zest, and lemon juice until well combined. Still pulsing, slowly add margarine through the feed tube.

4. Add the sour cream and vanilla and pulse to incorporate.

5. Add the wet ingredients to the bowl with the dry ingredients one-fourth at a time. Mix carefully by hand to combine; do not overmix.

6. Bake in the preheated oven for 65 minutes, or until a toothpick inserted in the middle of the loaf comes out clean. Remove from the oven and transfer to a wire rack. Allow to cool in the pan for 20 minutes.

For the Lemon Syrup

1. While the loaf is cooling, make the lemon syrup: Heat the lemon juice and sugar in a saucepan over medium heat for about 7 minutes, or until the sugar

is completely dissolved and a syrup has formed. Remove from the heat and set aside.

THE LEMON ICING
(OPTIONAL)

1 cup confectioners' sugar

4 tablespoons fresh
lemon juice

2. Line a large platter with parchment or wax paper and invert the loaf on the platter. Poke several holes on top (previously the bottom) of the loaf with a toothpick. Using a teaspoon, slowly drizzle the lemon syrup over the loaf. Give the syrup a chance to soak into the loaf between applications. If you are very careful, you may do the same with the sides of the loaf.

3. If you choose to ice your loaf, wait 20 more minutes to completely cool the cake before doing so.

For the Lemon Icing

1. Whisk together the confectioners' sugar and lemon juice. If the mixture is too stiff to spread, add more lemon juice, a teaspoonful at a time, and whisk again. If the mixture is too loose, add a small amount of sugar until you reach the desired consistency. I prefer mine to be thick.

2. Ice the cake. The icing will harden after about 15 minutes, but the loaf is equally delicious whether the icing is soft or hard.

Makes one 9 × 5-inch loaf; 10 slices

Classic Strawberry-Raspberry Bars

These bars are a classic, and I like to treat them that way. I cut them into big rectangles
and serve them on a glass platter with a doily. Vary the flavor of the preserves
as you choose for these delicious bars!

THE CRUST

1¼ cups all-purpose flour

½ cup dairy-free margarine, chilled

⅓ cup packed light brown sugar

THE TOPPING

½ cup all-purpose flour

½ cup packed light brown sugar

¼ cup dairy-free margarine, at room temperature

¾ teaspoon vanilla extract

THE FILLING

½ cup raspberry preserves

½ cup strawberry preserves

THE GLAZE

½ cup confectioners' sugar

½ teaspoon vanilla extract

Soy milk or rice milk

For the Crust

1. Preheat the oven to 350 degrees. Spray a 13 × 9-inch pan with nonstick baking spray. For thicker bars use a 9 × 9-inch pan.

2. Combine the flour, margarine, and brown sugar and mix at low speed, scraping the bowl (especially the bottom, as that is where the margarine settles) with a spatula often, until the ingredients are combined into a fine, crumbly mixture.

3. Press the mixture into the bottom of the prepared pan. Place a piece of wax paper on top, and press to evenly distribute the mixture. Bake the crust approximately 20 minutes, until edges are just lightly browned.

For the Topping

1. Combine the flour, brown sugar, margarine, and vanilla. Beat on low speed, scraping down the sides of the bowl often, until well mixed. Set aside.

For the Filling

1. In a small bowl, combine the raspberry and strawberry preserves with a spoon.

2. Spread the preserve mixture on the hot, partially baked crust, leaving ⅛ inch of the outer edge uncovered.

Sprinkle with the crumb topping. Return to the oven and continue baking for 20 to 25 minutes.

3. Cool the bars completely.

For the Glaze

1. Whisk the confectioners' sugar and vanilla in a small bowl. Stir in enough soy milk to reach a glaze consistency. Drizzle the glaze over the bars.

2. Once the glaze has set, cut into 3 × 2-inch bars and place on a doily-lined platter.

Makes twelve to sixteen 3 × 2-inch bars

Lemon (or Key Lime) Squares

These bars are so delicious and light. They can also easily morph into key lime bars by simply replacing the lemon juice with key lime juice.

THE CRUST

1¼ cups unbleached all-purpose flour

½ cup confectioners' sugar

¼ teaspoon salt

8 tablespoons dairy-free margarine

THE FILLING

1½ cups silken tofu, pureed

2 tablespoons cornstarch

1⅓ cups granulated sugar

3 tablespoons flour

⅔ cup freshly squeezed lemon or key lime juice (add 2 tablespoons more if you want the bars more sour)

¼ teaspoon salt

¼ cup lemon or key lime zest

confectioners' sugar

For the Crust

1. Preheat the oven to 350 degrees. Spray a 9 × 9-inch baking pan with nonstick baking spray.
2. In the bowl of an electric mixer beat the flour, confectioners' sugar, salt, and margarine on low speed until blended. Increase the speed to medium and beat until a dough forms, occasionally scraping down the bowl with a rubber spatula. The mixture will be crumbly—almost powdery.
3. Press the mixture into the bottom of the prepared pan. Place a piece of wax paper on top and press to evenly distribute. Bake the crust approximately 20 minutes, until edges are just lightly browned.

For the Filling

1. While the crust is baking, prepare the lemon (or key lime) filling. Place the tofu and cornstarch in a mini food processor and process for about 30 seconds until completely smooth. (If you don't have a food processor, beat the tofu in a mixing bowl with an electric mixer until smooth, add cornstarch to the tofu, and continue to beat until it has dissolved.)
2. Add the sugar to the beaten tofu mixture and beat until dissolved and smooth. Be sure to scrape down the sides of the bowl as you mix.

3. Add the flour, lemon juice, and salt. Beat and scrape the bowl intermittently for 2 minutes.

4. Pour the filling over the warm crust, and sprinkle lemon zest on top.

5. Bake in the preheated oven for 35 minutes, or until the filling is set and lightly golden. Transfer the pan to a wire rack. Cool the bars completely.

6. When cool, cut with a sharp knife into the desired-size pieces. I recommend sprinkling sugar on top at this point rather than before the bars have been cut. Place the confectioners' sugar in a sieve and shake liberally over completely cooled lemon squares.

Makes sixteen 2 × 2-inch squares

Gingersnaps

If you love ginger, this recipe is for you! These gingersnaps are a snap to make and I love that they bake into flat, crispy cookies. I like to stack these in jars and give them as hostess gifts.

2½ cups unbleached all-purpose flour

¼ cup ground ginger

1½ teaspoons ground cinnamon

1½ teaspoons baking soda

½ teaspoon salt

1½ teaspoons Ener-G Egg Replacer

2 tablespoons water

1 cup dairy-free margarine

1¼ cups packed dark brown sugar

¾ cup molasses

1. Preheat the oven to 400 degrees. Line two to three cookie sheets with parchment paper.

2. Sift the flour, ginger, cinnamon, baking soda, and salt together in a mixing bowl and set aside.

3. In a small bowl, whisk together the egg replacer and water until well dissolved and frothy. Set aside.

4. With an electric mixer, cream the margarine and brown sugar together in a mixing bowl on medium speed. Beat the egg replacer and molasses into the mixture and blend well on high speed. Be sure to scrape down the sides of the bowl to fully incorporate all the ingredients.

5. Add the dry mixture to the wet ingredients and mix well, scraping down the sides of the bowl and mixing until everything is well combined.

6. Cover the bowl with plastic wrap and place in the refrigerator for 15 minutes.

7. Scoop the batter onto the prepared cookie sheets with a teaspoon. Use the end of a butter knife to remove the cookie dough from the spoon onto the parchment paper. Place the scoops of dough 1 inch apart.

8. Return the mixing bowl with unscooped dough to the refrigerator until it is time to scoop more cookies.

9. Dip the palm of your hand in warm water, and press the unbaked cookies down flat to give them a round

shape. Bake the cookies in the preheated oven for 18 to 20 minutes, until edges just begin to turn light brown. Be absolutely sure to switch the cookie sheets between racks halfway through the baking time, so the bottom sheet of cookies doesn't burn! Remove the cookie sheets from the oven and place on a wire rack.

10. For crispier cookies, let the cookies cool directly on the baking sheet. For cookies that are still crispy, yet a bit softer, lift the parchment paper off the hot baking sheets and transfer to a cool surface. Remove the cookies from the parchment paper when they are firm and cool.

Makes 6 dozen 1½-inch cookies

Fruity Frozen Pie

I personally prefer to make this pie "regulation size" because it looks so pretty when sliced! When everyone sees how yummy and refreshing it looks, it will be gobbled up so quickly you won't have to worry about it melting!

1 pint vanilla dairy-free ice cream

1 cup frozen raspberries

1 pint fruit-flavored sorbet of your choice

½ cup dairy-free chocolate syrup (optional)

1 store-bought graham cracker crumb pie crust (read ingredient label carefully)

1 pint fresh raspberries

1 tablespoon sugar

1. Thaw the ice cream, raspberries, and sorbet at room temperature for 20 minutes until softened but not melted.

2. Meanwhile, if you want a chocolaty-flavored pie, spread chocolate syrup evenly over the bottom of the crust. Let set for 10 minutes in the freezer.

3. Scoop the thawed ice cream into the crust and spread evenly with a spatula. Place in freezer for 20 minutes to set.

4. In the meantime, put the frozen raspberries into a medium bowl and gently toss with the sugar.

5. Take the pie out of the freezer and sprinkle the berries in an even layer over the ice cream.

6. Spoon the sorbet on top to cover the whole pie.

7. Decorate the pie by placing fresh raspberries (open side down) around the perimeter of the pie top.

8. Return the pie to the freezer for 2 hours, or until ready to serve.

9. Slice the pie with a very sharp knife that has been dipped in a tall glass of warm water. Serve immediately.

Makes one 9-inch pie; 8 slices

Oh Fudge!

This is an amazing fudge recipe that I have shared with millions of Divvies fans on the back of our semisweet gourmet chocolate chip bags. This recipe makes enough for a party and then some. Send your guests home with little white bakery boxes of fudge, lined with parchment paper and tied up with a ribbon as a sweet reminder of the party.

1. Line a 9 × 9-inch pan with parchment paper or aluminum foil by placing two long sheets perpendicular to each other so they stick out of the sides of the pan, pushing the paper into the corners of the pan. This will make removing the finished fudge much neater.

2. Heat 2 cups of the sugar, the margarine, liquid creamer, and salt in a saucepan over medium heat on stovetop. Stir constantly.

3. Remove the saucepan from the heat, add the chips, and stir for 2 minutes until the chocolate is melted and the mixture is smooth.

4. Add the vanilla and the remaining ¼ cup of sugar. Stir until the sugar is dissolved and the mixture is smooth.

5. Pour the melted fudge into the prepared pans.

6. Press marshmallows and/or peppermint onto the top of the fudge, if desired.

7. Let the fudge cool in the refrigerator for 1 to 2 hours until solid. Remove the fudge from the pan by lifting the ends of the parchment paper. Place the fudge, still on the paper, on a flat countertop. With a very sharp knife, cut the fudge into 2 × 1-inch pieces.

Makes eighteen 2 × 1-inch pieces

2¼ cups sugar

½ cup dairy-free margarine

½ cup Silk dairy-free liquid soy creamer

⅛ teaspoon salt

2 cups Divvies Semisweet Chocolate Chips (2¼ cups for real chocoholics)

½ teaspoon vanilla extract

THE TOPPINGS (OPTIONAL)

Mini marshmallows

Peppermint candies, broken into bite-size pieces

Chocolate chips

Chocolate Fountain with Dippers

I love this dessert because it is so interactive (messy, but fun!). If you use a safe gourmet chocolate, like Divvies semisweet chocolate, everyone can dive in with their dippers of choice. I highly recommend that you purchase a chocolate fountain of your very own.

2 to 5 pounds of Divvies Semisweet Chocolate Chips (depending on how much your fountain can handle and how many people you are serving)

½ cup canola oil

DIPPER IDEAS

Whole strawberries

Banana slices

Cubes of vanilla cake

Cubes of chocolate cake

Cubes of banana bread

Pretzels

Marshmallows

Pineapple

1. Follow the instructions that come with your chocolate fountain, or follow the steps below (which may also be done in a bowl).

2. Fill a microwave-safe bowl with the chocolate chips and canola oil (about ½ cup of oil per 5 pounds of chocolate).

3. Place the bowl of chips and oil into the microwave and cook on high for about 2 minutes. Remove the bowl from the microwave and stir the partially melted chocolate.

4. Return the bowl to the microwave and cook on high again for another minute. Remove the bowl and carefully stir to completely melt the chocolate. If necessary, heat for a few more seconds until the chocolate is completely melted and smooth.

5. Turn your fountain on. (Be sure to read the instructions—some fountains need to be preheated.)

6. Carefully pour the warm melted chocolate from the bowl directly into the bowl portion of the chocolate fountain until the fountain is loaded.

7. As the auger starts, the chocolate will begin to flow through the fountain, covering and warming the tiers.

8. After a few minutes of operating, the chocolate flow should be consistent. If the chocolate is still too thick, add more oil, a tablespoon at a time, to the bowl of chocolate to thin to the desired consistency.

Makes a fountain's worth of chocolate to feed a crowd

Working with Melted Chocolate

1. Always have bags of Divvies Semisweet Chocolate Chips on hand because this chocolate is free of any milk and nut contamination.

2. When working with melted chocolate, be certain that all bowls, tools, and equipment are completely dry. Chocolate and water (even a drop) do not mix. Microwaving chocolate is faster and easier than melting it in a double boiler. Use a microwave-safe bowl. Never microwave chocolate for too long as the chocolate will burn.

3. To avoid making a huge mess when melting chocolate in the microwave, use paper bowls. If you've ever attempted to wash a bowl that is coated in hardened chocolate, you know that the cleaning process can be very messy! When you are done, simply discard the bowls.

4. Do not reuse the same bowl that chocolate has already been melted in. This would cause the remaining chocolate from the previous batch to burn. Use a clean bowl each time you melt chocolate.

5. To melt chocolate in a double boiler, place the chips in the top portion of the double boiler and place over low heat, stirring occasionally, until the chocolate is melted. Make sure that absolutely no water from the bottom of the pan gets into the melting chocolate, or it will seize and separate.

"Brown" Chocolate Bags

Looking for a dessert that will really wow all your guests? It's in the bag. These individual chocolate bags look like little brown paper lunch sacks—too cute! You can fill them with sorbet and berries, or make a larger bag and fill it full of strawberries for a buffet table of desserts. Guests literally eat their way through these.

Several flat-bottomed, small, unused coffee-bean bags. They must have flat bottoms and the inside must have a plastic coating.

Small pastry brush, small spatula and spoon

¾ cup Divvies Semisweet Chocolate Chips per chocolate bag

2 tablespoons nut- and dairy-free chocolate sauce per chocolate bag

2 scoops raspberry dairy-free sorbet per chocolate bag (or flavor of your choice)

¼ pint raspberries per chocolate bag (or berries of your choice)

Fresh mint leaves (optional)

1. Cut the bags to 2 to 3 inches tall.

2. Melt the chocolate chips in a microwave-safe bowl. Microwave on high for 2 minutes. Remove the bowl and stir the chocolate so melted chips melt the unmelted ones. If necessary, microwave again in 15 second intervals. Be careful not to burn the chocolate.

3. With a small, dry pastry brush or icing spatula, paint the inside of each bag with melted chocolate. You may want to use the spatula and spoon to help with the painting. Start at the bottom and work up the sides. Make sure chocolate gets into all the corners. Be very generous with the chocolate, otherwise it will crack when you peel the paper bag.

4. Place the bag(s) on a flat surface such as a small cutting board or tray that will fit on a freezer shelf, or simply clear a freezer shelf and line it with aluminum foil.

5. Freeze the bags until the chocolate has completely hardened—at least half an hour. TAKE ONE BAG OUT OF THE FREEZER AT A TIME—you do not want the chocolate to begin to soften. Gently pull away the bag starting at the seams on the bottom.

6. To present the chocolate bags as dessert, drizzle chocolate sauce on each serving plate just before serving,

place a chocolate bag on top, and fill each bag with scoops of sorbet. Sprinkle berries in the bags and on the plates. Garnish the sorbet with mint leaves if desired.

Makes 1 bag

Make extra bags! You can store chocolate bags in a safe section of your freezer and have them ready for a special occasion. During the cooler months, fill the bags with wrapped hard candies, wrap in cellophane, and tie with a ribbon—a very special gift!

Warm Indie Chocolate Puddings

This is my friend Justine's recipe for warm, decadent chocolate pudding pie. Justine is the co-owner of Pisces Café in Babylon, New York. As well as an eatery, Pisces Café is an independent arts venue, thus the "Indie" in the name of this recipe. She says all of her customers love this indulgent dessert, and we think you will, too!

4 Andrea's Mom's Granola Bars (recipe page 104)

One 12.3-ounce box shelf stable (not refrigerated) firm tofu such as Mori-Nu Silken Tofu

⅛ teaspoon salt

¼ teaspoon vanilla extract

One 12-ounce bag Divvies Semisweet Chocolate Chips

2 tablespoons cocoa powder

1. Set out five small bowls. Cut three granola bars into five 2-inch pieces. Place one piece at the bottom of each bowl. Break up the fourth bar into small pieces and set aside to use as garnish.

2. Beat together the tofu, salt, and vanilla in an electric mixer, until the tofu is well-broken down.

3. Melt the chocolate chips in a microwave-safe bowl on high power in the microwave for 1 minute. Remove from microwave and stir the chips until melted. If necessary, microwave in additional 15-second intervals until the chips are entirely melted.

4. Pour the melted chocolate into the mixing bowl with the tofu and beat together on medium-high speed until creamy.

5. Add the cocoa powder and blend quickly until just incorporated.

6. Quickly spoon the pudding equally into each bowl.

7. Garnish each pudding with a sprinkling of the reserved granola bar pieces, if desired.

8. Serve the puddings immediately while still warm. Leftovers may be refrigerated and served cold the next day.

Makes five 5-ounce puddings

Choose-Your-Own-Mix-In Scones

If you serve these scones hot out of the oven, you'd think you were serving banana splits to kindergartners! I prepare the dough ahead of time, and when dinner is winding down, I pop them in the oven. The smell alone draws everyone to the kitchen and we eat our piping-hot scones gathered around the counter. They rarely make it to the table!

1. Preheat the oven to 350 degrees. Line a cookie sheet with parchment paper and set aside.

2. Stir the lemon juice into the soy milk and set aside; the lemon juice acts as a thickening agent.

3. Mix the 2 teaspoons of sugar and cinnamon together in a small bowl and set aside.

4. Whisk the flour, cornmeal, ¼ cup of sugar, baking powder, baking soda, and salt in a large mixing bowl. Set aside.

5. In a separate small mixing bowl, whisk together the melted margarine, soy milk and lemon mixture, and vanilla.

6. Add the wet ingredients to the dry ingredients. Stir with a large spoon, being careful to scrape down the sides of the bowl, and incorporate all the ingredients well.

7. Add the berries and/or chips to the batter and gently stir. I sometimes make a variety of scones by dividing the scone batter into smaller bowls, and adding different mix-ins.

8. Scoop 12 scones onto the lined cookie sheets. Sprinkle each scone with a generous amount of the sugar-cinnamon mixture.

¼ tablespoon freshly squeezed lemon juice

⅓ cup soy milk

¼ cup plus 2 teaspoons sugar

⅛ teaspoon ground cinnamon

1 cup unbleached all-purpose flour

2 tablespoons stone-ground cornmeal

2 teaspoons baking powder

¼ teaspoon baking soda

¼ teaspoon salt

4 tablespoons melted dairy-free margarine

½ teaspoon vanilla extract

Your choice of raspberries, blueberries, and/or Divvies Semisweet Chocolate Chips

9. Bake the scones in the preheated oven for 15 to 18 minutes, or until the bottom edges are golden brown. Test by inserting a toothpick into the center of a scone; when it comes out clean, the scones are done. Remove from oven and eat while still warm.

Makes one dozen 4-inch scones

The Liquidity Factor

Keep everyone in the mix and the fun overflowing.

I have noticed that when kids are given some fun "tasks" to lend a hand at a party, they become a lot more involved in the event, and a lot less concerned about where they fit in. I gave Benjamin the job of taking care of everyone's drinks at a party we hosted at our home. He made it look like so much fun, so other kids his age jumped right in. It soon became a tradition at our parties—an activity that made all the kids feel included, taking the focus off what everyone was eating or not eating, and letting them tap their creative juices to concoct some pretty great (nonalcoholic) drinks.

The Setup (the kids should do this part, too!)

- *Create drink tickets*
- *Fill ice buckets*
- *Set out glassware*
- *Organize soft drinks and other bottled beverages*
- *Put out paperware and straws (try using hollow licorice— cut off both ends for an edible straw)*
- *Slice and arrange fruit (this may need adult supervision)*

Some kids who have food allergies do not feel comfortable with the idea of cooking and coming into contact with foods they are not familiar with (even if they aren't allergic to them). That used to be the case with Benjamin. I'm pretty sure by playing "bartender" and concocting drinks, his comfort level with experimenting was transferred to other safe foods.

THE DRINKS

Grape Soda

Everyone enjoys this healthy version!

Ice
½ cup seltzer
½ cup grape juice (you may want to choose white grape juice in case of a spill)

1. Fill a glass halfway with seltzer.
2. Slowly add grape juice until it reaches 1 inch below the top of the glass. Add ice.
3. Serve immediately.

Cherry Spritzer

This is very refreshing and a fun change from the juices in most spritzers.

Ice
½ cup cherry juice
1 cup sparkling mineral water or seltzer

1. Fill a glass with ice.
2. Pour the cherry juice over the ice and add the mineral water or seltzer and serve immediately.

Teamonade

This drink has been referred to by several names; I love "Teamonade" because that's what Adam's summer camp calls it.

4 cups iced tea
4 cups lemonade
Lemon slices (optional)
Mint leaves (optional)
Ice
Tall glasses

1. Fill a pitcher halfway with iced tea. Fill the remainder with lemonade.
2. Add the lemon slices and/or mint leaves if desired.
3. Pour over ice in a tall glass and serve immediately.

Hot-Mulled Apple Cider

On cold days, everyone enjoys the cinnamon-y scent of hot-mulled cider simmering on the stove. We love greeting guests with a soothing hot mug full of this delicious treat.

½ gallon apple cider
2 cinnamon sticks
7 whole cloves
⅛ teaspoon ground nutmeg (optional)
⅛ teaspoon ground allspice (optional)

1. Combine all the ingredients in a saucepan.
2. Place over medium heat and bring to a boil. Reduce the heat to low and simmer for 15 minutes.
3. Serve piping hot in mugs.

Root Beer Float

For everyone who just can't get enough of those erupting baking soda–volcano science fair projects, these drinks are for you! Wow your crowd by putting the nondairy "ice cream" in the root beer at the last minute so they can enjoy the full fizz effect.

Tall drinking glass
1 scoop vanilla nondairy ice cream
Ice-cold root beer soda
Straw
Long-stemmed parfait spoon

1. Set a tall drinking glass on a small plate to protect the table from overflowing root beer. Place a large scoop of vanilla ice cream in the glass.
2. Slowly fill the glass three-quarters full with root beer. The ice cream will float into the root beer and fizz.
3. Serve the floats with straws and parfait spoons.

Quadruple-Fruity Punch with Cherry Orange Ice Ring

This recipe makes so much, you need a punch bowl. I recommend you make and freeze the ice ring ahead of time. Then prepare the punch just before adding the ice ring and serving.

THE ICE RING

7 maraschino cherries
1 medium navel orange, thinly sliced
1 small lemon, thinly sliced
5-cup ring mold
4 cups water

1. Arrange fruit as you choose in a 5-cup ring mold and add water until mold is full.
2. Place the mold in the freezer and freeze until solid.

THE PUNCH (MEASUREMENTS NEED NOT BE EXACT)

1 pint raspberries or sliced strawberries or both
1½ gallons pineapple juice
1½ gallons orange juice
1½ gallons lemonade
1½ gallons cranberry juice
1 cup canned or fresh pineapple chunks

1. Place the raspberries and/or strawberries in the punch bowl.
2. Pour all the juices into the bowl.
3. Add the pineapple.
4. Gently stir very well to combine the juices.
5. Chill in the fridge until ready to serve.
6. Just before serving unmold the ice ring by wrapping the bottom of the mold in a hot, damp dishcloth. Invert the ring onto a baking sheet or other clean surface, then place fruit side up in the punch bowl.

Super-Cool Soda

Ramune (which means *carbonated* in Japanese) is a really unique soft drink. You may receive a trophy for serving this! It used to be served only at specialty Asian markets, but lately I've been seeing it at gourmet grocery stores (near the sushi station).

We served Ramune to thirty boys at our son Adam's ninth birthday sleepover party—I know, thirty boys, what were we thinking? They went crazy for this soda because it tastes like super-sweet lemon-lime soda; and it was an experience just to open the bottle!

To open a bottle of Ramune, you have to remove the top, pop out a small plastic plunger from its casing, and then use the plunger to pop out a marble that seals the opening of the bottle. The neck of the bottle has two indentations that hold the marble when you tip the bottle back to drink from it. The opening of the bottle is much too small for the marble to escape and flow into your mouth, so this is not a choking hazard. It's just a very cool drink!

SWEETS
THAT MAKE THE
SCHOOLHOUSE
ROCK

Extra Credit to All who Bring these Treats to Class!

Working WITH the System 101

Perhaps nothing delights a child more than the sight of a big platter of treats arriving through his classroom door to break up the rhythm of the day (as unexpected and exciting as an electric guitar solo breaking out in the middle of a Bach concerto). And if those treats arrive in the arms of *his* parents, well, then suddenly he is the rock star and this is *his* solo!

This impressive spread, should, of course, be safe for everyone in the classroom to enjoy. While getting parents to understand the importance of bringing allergen-free treats that everyone can share may be tricky, kids, on the other hand, are actually very quick studies when it comes to finding ways to include their friends. Many parents have told us that their children ask them to pack "safe" lunches so they don't have to worry about cross-contamination when they sit at the same lunch table as Benjamin.

Up until the third grade, Benjamin's classmates often asked him why he couldn't eat certain foods. This just made me more determined in my efforts to be there for him with delicious treats the whole class could share. I even brought in safe, packaged snacks to the school nurse's office in case *any* child forgot to bring a snack from home. When dealing with the subject of class snacks and celebrations, make sure you approach the teachers and staff at your child's school with an open mind and a huge dose of patience—both will take you a long way in making school pleasant for your child.

- Talk to your child's teacher when the school year starts to establish a good relationship.
- Ask for a calendar of celebrations and classroom projects involving food.
- Make sure you have a few safe treats stored in the school's freezer.
- Share your recipes and resources for store-bought safe treats with the teacher and the parents of your child's classmates.

The Cupcake Alternative

Cupcakes are tried-and-true crowd-pleasers, but if you bring in an unexpected treat for the next big celebration, the kids will be extra excited.

Case in point: Benjamin's school birthday celebrations have always been unconventional. His favorite food in the world is, believe it or not, white rice from our favorite Chinese food restaurant. So, instead of birthday cake, I bring in small cartons of white rice for each student and teacher in his class. By now, all the students are familiar with the tradition and look forward to it every year. The rice is totally allergen-free, and I make sure the brand of soy sauce I bring is gluten-free for anyone who is sensitive to gluten.

Rice not your thing? Why not try . . .

- Ice Pops (if you are sending them in the morning, make sure they can be stored in a freezer)
- Marshmallow Treats
- Brownies
- Cookies
- Chocolate-Covered Marshmallows
- Chocolate-Covered Strawberries
- Chocolate-Covered Pretzels
- Muffins for a morning party
- Fruit Kabobs
- Nonfood items such as stickers, bouncy balls, smelly markers, friendship bracelets, bandanas, fake tattoos, etc.

Bake Sale—Divvies Style!

Get your group to steer away from serving only store-bought items. People love to buy homemade and will pay much more for it than they will for the same items they see in the grocery store. Feature "celebrity" bakers in a clever way—like the teachers, the principal, and the coaches. Label everything clearly, listing all ingredients and potential allergens.

- Come up with a theme, perhaps based on what you are raising money for: That usually gets bakers excited to take up the challenge and tweak their favorite recipes just a bit to fit the theme. Or just simply wrap them to the chosen theme.
- E-mail all potential bakers with ideas and recipes that fit the theme in case they are struggling to come up with something.
- Set up a separate section for allergen-free treats. Make sure this area is just as festive and has just as many delicious and decadent choices. The only difference between the tables should be the ingredients contained in the goodies.

Hot Sellers

- Extra-Thick, Treasure-Filled Marshmallow Treats
- Chocolate-Dipped Candy Shop Pretzel Sticks
- Chocolaty, Chewy Brownies
- Benjamin's Chocolate Chip Cookies
- Divvies Famous Chocolate Cupcakes
- Mini Loaves of Banana Bread
- Oh Fudge!
- Gummy Candy Squish Kabobs

The Art of Baking

Why not step out of the box and get creative with your next bake sale? One fun idea is to raise money for the art programs at your child's school. You can assign a famous artist to each baker so they can get creative with their treats:

Seurat's *Cupcake in Pointillist Sprinkles (page 59)*

Van Gogh's *Starry Lemon Squares (page 34)*

Gauguin's *Marshmallow Treats (page 106)*

Dali's *Chocolate-Dipped Pretzel Sticks (page 132)*

Everyone will rise to the occasion and the bake sale tables will look great (as opposed to a sea of plastic wrap), all while promoting a great cause.

Divvies Famous Chocolate Cupcakes

Bake the now-famous cupcakes that Benjamin (the inspiration behind Divvies) and I made in front of millions of national TV viewers on The Martha Stewart Show. You won't believe how moist and delicious these are!

1½ cups unbleached flour

¾ cup sugar

¼ cup cocoa powder

1 teaspoon baking soda

½ teaspoon salt

5 tablespoons vegetable oil

1 tablespoon white vinegar

1¼ cups water

1. Preheat the oven to 350 degrees. Line a 12-well cupcake pan with paper liners.

2. In a mixing bowl, whisk the flour, sugar, cocoa, baking soda, and salt together until well combined; do not sift. Set aside.

3. In a large mixing bowl combine the vegetable oil, vinegar, and water and blend with an electric mixer on medium speed.

4. Add the dry ingredients to the liquid ingredients and mix until very smooth, scraping batter from sides and bottom of bowl with a spatula. Continue to mix until all the ingredients are well incorporated. This batter will be more watery than typical cake batters.

5. Pour the batter into the lined cupcake pan filling each well about three-quarters full.

6. Bake the cupcakes for 25 minutes on the center rack of the preheated oven. After 12 minutes, rotate the pan to ensure more even baking. Remove the cupcake pan from the oven, and immediately transfer the cupcakes to a wire cooling rack—this is very important as it allows excess moisture to evaporate from the bottom of the paper baking cups.

Makes 1 dozen cupcakes

> *The sky is the limit when it comes to decorating cupcakes. Look for nut- and dairy-free sprinkles, colored sugars, Divvies chocolate chips, candies, etc. to make cupcakes fun and festive! And don't forget, you can freeze unfrosted cupcakes so you always have something special on hand for last minute occasions.*

Vanilla Cupcakes

1. Preheat the oven to 350 degrees. Line a 12-well cupcake pan with paper liners.

2. Whisk together the cake flour, baking powder, and salt. Set aside.

3. Emulsify the egg replacer and seltzer in a small bowl using a small whisk until frothy. Set aside.

4. In the bowl of an electric mixer, with the mixer on high speed, beat the softened margarine, sugar, vanilla, and egg replacer until fluffy. At least twice during the mixing, scrape down the sides and bottom of the bowl thoroughly in order to fully incorporate all the ingredients.

5. Add the flour mixture and soy milk to the sugar mixture, alternately, ¼ cup at a time. Mix on medium speed, scraping the sides and bottom of bowl, until just incorporated. Do not overmix or the batter will be stiff.

6. Distribute and spread the batter evenly among the paper liners.

7. Bake the cupcakes for 18 to 20 minutes in the preheated oven. The cupcakes are fully baked when a toothpick inserted in the middle comes out clean.

8. Cool the cupcakes for 10 minutes in the pan, then transfer to wire cooling racks. Cool completely before frosting or adding fillings.

Makes 18 cupcakes

2½ cups cake flour

2½ tablespoons baking powder

½ teaspoon salt

1½ teaspoons Ener-G Egg Replacer

2 tablespoons unflavored seltzer

½ cup dairy-free margarine, softened

1¼ cups sugar

1½ teaspoons vanilla extract

½ cup plus 2 tablespoons soy milk

Chocolate Frosting

2 cups confectioners'
sugar

½ cup cocoa powder

⅛ teaspoon salt

1 cup dairy-free margarine

1 teaspoon vanilla extract

¼ cup soy milk or rice milk

1. Whisk together the unsifted confectioners' sugar, unsifted cocoa, and salt. Set aside.

2. Cream the margarine and vanilla in a mixing bowl with an electric mixer on medium speed.

3. Scrape down the sides of the mixing bowl with a spatula, then add the sugar mixture ½ cup at a time, and simultaneously, the soy milk 1 tablespoon at a time. Continue beating on medium speed until all the ingredients are well incorporated and the frosting is smooth and creamy. If you prefer a thinner consistency, add more soy milk, a teaspoon at a time.

Makes 2¼ cups frosting

Flower-Power Cupcake Tower!

Create a tower by holding up three tiers of plates, in graduated sizes, with overturned glasses. Place decorated cupcakes around the two lower tiers. Place one cupcake with a candle atop the highest tier, and fill in the space around the cupcake with Divvies Gourmet Jelly Beans.

To decorate the cupcakes, cut Divvies Gourmet Jelly Beans in half to create flower petals; in quarters to create leaves; and in tiny pieces to create flower centers. Carefully press the jelly beans into the cupcake in a flower pattern.

Vanilla Frosting

1. Combine the 1¼ cups of unsifted confectioners' sugar, margarine, salt, and vanilla in a mixing bowl and beat on medium speed. Scrape down the sides of the mixing bowl with a spatula, and continue to mix for 1 minute.

2. Add the rice milk and continue mixing on medium speed. With the mixer running, slowly add the remaining ½ cup confectioners' sugar until you achieve the desired sweetness. Beat for an additional 4 to 5 minutes, until creamy.

3. Frost cooled cupcakes or cake.

Makes 2 cups

1¼ cups plus ½ cup unsifted confectioners' sugar,

½ cup dairy-free margarine, chilled

⅛ teaspoon salt

½ teaspoon vanilla extract

2 tablespoons rice milk

If you don't have time to make frosting from scratch, keep Divvies chocolate and vanilla frostings on hand. We make the vanilla frosting in a variety of beautiful pastel colors.

Chocolaty, Chewy Brownies

Benjamin and I made this recipe on CBS's The Early Show. As soon as the show was over and the platter of brownies was moved off the set to the studio's prep kitchen, many of the show's staff charged in for the brownie they had been craving all morning! I love this recipe because by adjusting the baking time, you can easily "customize" the brownies' consistency from gooey to chewy to cakey.

1¾ cups all-purpose flour

¾ cup cocoa powder

1 teaspoon baking soda

½ teaspoon salt

1¾ cups sugar

⅓ cup canola oil

1 cup nondairy sour cream

2 tablespoons applesauce

¼ cup light corn syrup

1 teaspoon vanilla extract

2 teaspoons white vinegar

1 cup Divvies Semisweet Chocolate Chips

1. Preheat the oven to 350 degrees. Spray an 8 × 8-inch or 9 × 9-inch pan with nonstick baking spray.

2. Sift the flour, cocoa powder, baking powder, and salt into a bowl. Set aside.

3. Combine the sugar, oil, nondairy sour cream, applesauce, corn syrup, vanilla, and vinegar in a mixing bowl and, using an electric mixer, beat on medium speed until very smooth. Be sure to scrape down the sides of the bowl so all the ingredients are well incorporated.

4. Add the dry ingredients to the wet ingredients and beat on medium speed. Once again, be sure to scrape down the sides of the bowl with a spatula.

5. Fold in the chocolate chips, reserving ¼ cup to sprinkle on top once the brownies are baking, then mix on low speed until the chips are evenly distributed throughout the batter.

6. Pour the batter into the prepared pan. Use a spatula to distribute evenly.

7. Bake the brownies in the preheated oven for 40 to 50 minutes.

8. After the brownies have been baking for approximately 15 minutes, sprinkle the reserved ¼ cup of

chips evenly over the top of the brownies and re-
sume baking.

9. Rotate the pan halfway through the baking time.
Test the brownies with a toothpick for your pre-
ferred brownie consistency. The shorter the baking
time, the fudgier the brownie. The longer the baking time, the cakier the brownie.

10. Cool the brownies in the pan for at least 30 minutes
before serving.

11. Cut the brownies into 2 × 2-inch squares.

Makes sixteen 2 × 2-inch brownies

Variations: For chocolate-mint brownies, substitute
1½ cups of broken up bits of Divvies Benjamint Crunch
Bars for the chocolate chips.

For a decadent surprise the kids will love, mix the
brownie batter into dairy-free "ice cream" for "brownie
batter ice cream."

Popcorn Snowmen

Faster to create than a gingerbread house and more fun than holiday cookies, these sweet, sticky snowmen provide hours of creative, and yes, messy, fun. Be sure to have plenty of damp paper towels ready for greasy hands. This project is recommended for kids aged 8 and up, as the popcorn will crumble if the snowmen are not handled with care.

10 cups popped regular popcorn (or Divvies Kettle Corn)

One 10.5-ounce package marshmallows

1/4 cup dairy-free margarine (and a bit extra to "butter" very clean hands when forming "snowballs")

1 teaspoon vanilla extract

8 to 12 small thick pretzel sticks

DECORATIONS

Peanut-, tree nut-, milk-, egg-free sprinkles

Licorice

Gum drops

Cinnamon candies

1. Spray a large spoon and a large bowl with nonstick cooking spray, or grease with margarine.
2. Place the popcorn in a large bowl and set aside.
3. Melt the marshmallows and margarine in a large saucepan over low heat, stirring frequently. Remove the pan from heat and stir in the vanilla. Let stand for a few minutes to cool.
4. Pour the melted marshmallow mixture over the popcorn. With the large prepared spoon, stir to evenly coat.
5. Coat your palms with margarine and form the popcorn-marshmallow mixture into "snowballs" by rolling in your hands and packing tightly.
6. Place the balls on parchment paper and set aside for a few minutes until they are set and hold their shape.
7. Stick 1/2 pretzel into one ball. If the ball loosens, simply mold it back with your hands.
8. Attach a second ball to the top half of the pretzel to form a snowman. Again, press the ball back together if it loosens and press the two balls together.
9. Decorate as desired with various confections. Of course, you can serve these as individual popcorn balls, if you wish.

Makes eight 6-inch snowmen

Benjamin's Chocolate Chip Cookies

This is my signature chocolate chip cookie recipe that convinced me of the fact that no one has to be left out of sharing delicious sweets. These cookies usually go directly from the oven to the mouths of my three boys and all their friends. They never have time to cool, much less make it to the cookie jar! These cookies were the original inspiration for the whole line of Divvies treats, so they are very dear to my heart.

1. Preheat the oven to 350 degrees. Line three cookie sheets with parchment paper.

2. In a large bowl, whisk together flour, baking soda, and salt. Set aside.

3. In a small bowl, whisk the egg replacer with the water until well dissolved. Set aside.

4. In a mixing bowl, beat margarine and sugars with an electric mixer on high speed until just fluffy. Be sure to scrape down the sides of the bowl with a spatula and continue to mix.

5. Add the pureed tofu, egg replacer, and vanilla to the mixing bowl. Mix until well combined, scraping down the sides of the mixing bowl.

6. Add the flour mixture to the wet ingredients and mix until well incorporated. Fold in 1¾ cups of the chocolate chips by hand, and be certain not to over-mix the dough.

7. Scoop the cookie dough with a #24 ice-cream scooper, and place the scoops 2 inches apart on the parchment paper–lined cookie sheets. Flatten each scoop slightly with your hand.

8. Bake the cookies in the preheated oven for 18 to 20 minutes, rotating the cookie sheets halfway through

2 cups all-purpose flour

1 teaspoon baking soda

½ teaspoon salt

1½ teaspoons Ener-G Egg Replacer

2 tablespoons water

1 cup dairy-free margarine

¾ cup granulated sugar

¾ cup packed dark brown sugar

¼ cup silken tofu, pureed

2 teaspoons vanilla extract

2 cups Divvies Semisweet Chocolate Chips

baking time, until the edges begin to turn golden.

9. After the cookies have been baking for about 5 minutes, distribute the remaining ¼ cup of chocolate chips among the cookies, placing a few on top of each.

10. Cool the cookies directly on the baking sheets.

Makes two dozen 3-inch cookies

Variation: Mix chocolate chip cookie dough into dairy-free "ice cream" for a chocolate chip–cookie dough frozen treat. The kids will be psyched!

You can keep pureed tofu in the refrigerator in an airtight container. Just be sure to remove the excess water before using it in a recipe.

Strawberry-Rhubarb Oatmeal Cookies

I love that these cookies are not too sweet, yet so satisfying, plus the crisped rice gives them a nice texture. I prefer to use a more tart preserve such as strawberry-rhubarb or sour cherry. The light color of the cookies paired with the red of the preserves looks so pretty.

1. Preheat the oven to 400 degrees. Line three cookie sheets with parchment paper.

2. In a mixing bowl, combine the flour, oats, baking soda, and baking powder. Set aside.

3. With an electric mixer on medium speed, beat the granulated and brown sugars and margarine together until fluffy. Add the water, vanilla, and oil. Continue to beat until well combined, scraping down the sides of the mixing bowl to fully incorporate all the ingredients.

4. Slowly add the flour-oat mixture in ½ cup increments and mix on medium speed. Be sure to scrape the sides of the bowl intermittently.

5. Add the crisped rice cereal and mix on low speed.

6. Using a #24 scoop, scoop the dough in tablespoon-sized balls onto the lined baking sheets and lightly flatten with the palm of your hand. Leave about 1 inch between each cookie. With your fingertip, make 5 prints in the center of each cookie, creating the shape of a flower, and fill with preserves, about 1 teaspoon.

7. Bake the cookies in the preheated oven for 12 minutes, rotating the baking sheets halfway through the baking time, until the cookies are golden.

8. Cool cookies on the cookie sheets before serving.

Makes sixteen 3-inch cookies

3 cups unbleached flour

2 cups thick-cut oats (quick oats work, too)

1 teaspoon baking soda

1 teaspoon baking powder

¾ cup granulated sugar (1 cup if you want them sweeter)

1 cup firmly packed light brown sugar

1 cup dairy-free margarine, at room temperature

½ cup water

1 teaspoon vanilla extract

3 tablespoons canola oil

1½ cups crisped rice cereal such as Rice Krispies

1¼ cup strawberry-rhubarb or sour cherry preserves (or any flavor you desire)

Blondies (Our Way)

These blondies are done the Divvies way—just a little bit different from the usual!

2⅓ cups unbleached flour

1 teaspoon baking soda

½ teaspoon baking powder

½ teaspoon salt

2 cups thick-cut rolled oats (quick or old-fashioned work, too)

1 cup dairy-free margarine

1 cup granulated sugar

1¼ cups packed brown sugar

½ cup silken tofu, pureed

1 teaspoon vanilla extract

1 cup Divvies Semisweet Chocolate Chips

1 cup Divvies BingGo! Divvine Chocolate Bar broken into ½-inch pieces

¾ cup miniature marshmallows, optional

1. Preheat the oven to 350 degrees. Spray a 9×9-inch pan (for thick blondies) or a 13×9-inch pan (for thinner blondies) with nonstick baking spray.

2. Whisk together the flour, baking soda, baking powder, salt, and oats in a large mixing bowl. Set aside.

3. Beat the margarine, sugars, tofu, and vanilla on medium speed. Scrape down the sides of the bowl, and continue mixing until well incorporated.

4. Add the dry ingredients, one-third at a time, to the margarine-sugar mixture. Scrape down the sides of the bowl, and continue to mix until well incorporated.

5. Add the chocolate chips, chocolate pieces, and marshmallows (if using), and mix on low speed until distributed evenly throughout the batter.

6. Pour the batter into the prepared baking pan and bake on the center rack of the preheated oven for about 30 minutes. Be sure to rotate the pan halfway through the baking time. Test for doneness with a sharp knife or toothpick.

Makes twelve to eighteen 3×2-inch blondies

(depending on pan size)

Chocolate Chip–Pumpkin Muffins and Loaves

Some kids turn their noses up when they find out their muffins are made with pumpkin, as it sounds like a devious adult plan to get them to eat vegetables. Add chocolate chips to the mix, and you'll have them eating these right out of your hand. If you make this recipe as a loaf, enjoy it sliced and toasted with dairy-free margarine or your favorite preserves.

1. Preheat the oven to 375 degrees. Line two 12-well cupcake pans with paper liners, or spray three 9 × 5-inch loaf pans or five 5 × 3-inch mini loaf pans with nonstick baking spray. For a variety, make both loaves and muffins.

2. Whisk together the flour, baking soda, salt, cinnamon, nutmeg, cloves, and ginger in a medium bowl. Set aside.

3. Place the pumpkin in a mixing bowl and beat with an electric mixer until pureed. Add the applesauce, canola oil, water, and sugars, and continue beating until the sugar has dissolved and all the ingredients are well combined.

4. Add the dry ingredients to the wet ingredient mixture. Beat together on medium speed. Be sure to thoroughly scrape down the sides of the bowl and the mixing paddle in order to incorporate all the ingredients. Continue beating for another minute. If there are lumps of dry flour in the batter, scrape down the sides of the bowl and mix one more time.

5. These loaves are delicious plain and simple, but if you choose to add a mix-in (or two!) you should add 1 cup total.

3½ cups all-purpose flour

2 teaspoons baking soda

1½ teaspoons salt

1 teaspoon ground cinnamon

1 teaspoon ground nutmeg

½ teaspoon ground cloves

½ teaspoon ground ginger

One 15-ounce can 100 percent pure pumpkin

1 cup applesauce

1 cup canola oil

⅓ cup water

3 cups granulated sugar

½ cup packed dark brown sugar, for sprinkling on top

1 cup Divvies Semisweet
Chocolate Chips

1 cup raisins

1 cup dried cranberries

1 cup peeled and chopped
apples

½ cup bran

These pumpkin loaves make a great gift during the fall season. Simply wrap and write your own ingredient label. You will really wow the crowd when they learn these are made without eggs or butter.

6. Fill the pan(s) with the batter. Lightly sprinkle a thin layer of brown sugar over tops of loaves and muffins.

7. Bake the muffins in the preheated oven for 24 to 26 minutes; mini loaves for 45 minutes; and large loaves range in baking time from 65 to 80 minutes. If chopped apples are added, the baking time may be a bit longer. Be sure to test for doneness by inserting a toothpick or sharp knife in the middle of the loaves or muffins. If it comes out clean, they are ready to come out of the oven.

8. Remove from oven and place the pans on wire racks. Let muffins cool for 10 minutes and loaves for 20 minutes; they will continue to bake a bit during this time. Then remove from pan so they do not overbake.

Makes 18 muffins or two 9 × 5-inch loaves

Breakfast in Your Cookie

. . . much better than having breakfast on your face! My son Max enjoys this as a mid-morning snack. These are soft like a chewy granola bar disguised as a cookie. They are great for a school party before lunch.

1. Preheat the oven to 400 degrees. Line three baking sheets with parchment paper.

2. In a small bowl, crush the graham cereal into small pieces; do not smash them into dust! Set aside.

3. Whisk together the flour, baking powder, baking soda, and salt in a medium mixing bowl and set aside.

4. Cream the margarine, brown sugar, tofu, apple juice, and vanilla in a mixing bowl with an electric mixer on medium speed until creamy. Be sure to scrape down the sides of the bowl with a spatula.

5. Add the flour mixture to the creamed ingredients in the mixing bowl and continue beating on medium speed until blended, scraping down the sides of the bowl and continuing to mix.

6. Add the oats, mixing on medium speed and scraping the sides of the bowl well.

7. Add the chocolate chips, apples, and raisins. Mix on low speed until well combined.

8. Scoop the dough with a #24 size scoop, then roll the scooped dough balls one at a time in the graham cereal crumbs so each ball is covered with crumbs. Place on the prepared baking sheet, 1 inch apart. Flatten each ball of dough by lightly pressing on the top.

2 cups crushed graham cereal

1½ cups all-purpose flour

1 teaspoon baking powder

1 teaspoon baking soda

¼ teaspoon salt

¾ cup dairy-free margarine, softened to room temperature

1 cup packed light brown sugar

¼ cup silken tofu, pureed

3 teaspoons apple juice

½ teaspoon vanilla extract

1½ cups quick-cooking oats

1⅓ cups Divvies Semisweet Chocolate Chips

1 medium apple, peeled, cored, and chopped into very small pieces

½ cup raisins

Place 1 to 2 cookies on a microwave-safe plate and set on high for 15 seconds. Enjoy these cookies for breakfast when they are warm and soft.

9. Bake the cookies in the preheated oven for about 15 minutes, rotating the pans and switching the racks halfway through the baking time. Cool the cookies on the baking sheets.

Makes eighteen 2-inch cookies

Frozen Cookie Dough to the Rescue

Having frozen cookie dough on hand will earn you a snack survival badge (and you can store cookie dough in an airtight container in the freezer for up to two months!). Just follow these simple steps:

1. Defrost the cookie dough for a couple of hours before you plan to bake. (For cookies made with oatmeal, add about ¼ cup of water into the dough once defrosted, as the oatmeal tends to absorb moisture during the freezing process.)

2. Preheat the oven to 350 degrees.

3. Scoop thawed cookie dough onto baking sheets lined with parchment paper, spacing them 1½ inches apart.

4. Bake the cookies for about 20 minutes. You may need to carefully monitor the first batch to determine the perfect baking time. After the first 10 minutes, rotate the baking sheet and switch oven racks to ensure even baking. The cookies are done when they're just turning golden brown on the edges.

5. Cool the cookies on baking sheets for 5 minutes. Transfer the cookies to wire racks to finish cooling.

Your Favorite Applesauce

Once you've made this applesauce you may never go back to store-bought again. It's easy to prepare and delicious, especially in the fall when apples are at their peak—and you can choose your favorite variety! Make a large quantity and freeze the applesauce in individual containers that can double as mini ice packs in your child's lunch box.

1. Peel and core the apples. Cut each apple into 1-inch cubes, place in a large saucepan, along with the cinnamon sticks, and set over low heat. The smaller the pieces of apple, the quicker they will become applesauce. Other fruit may be added to the pan at this time as well.

2. Keep the heat on low and stir frequently. (If you don't, you will need to add more water so the apples don't burn.) Use a masher to break up and mash pieces of fruit as they cook. Add sugar to your desired level of sweetness.

3. Cook until the applesauce reaches the texture you like. If you prefer your applesauce very smooth, puree with a hand-held blender once the apples have cooked.

Makes 5 cups sauce

3 pounds apples, your favorite variety

¼ cup water

2 cinnamon sticks

1 cup of berries, such as strawberries and blueberries; or 1 cup peeled and diced pears, peaches, and/or plums; or ½ cup dried cranberries or raisins (optional)

½ cup sugar

Chocolate-Covered Strawberries and Marshmallows

Whenever I make these, I make a ton—they really impress a crowd. This recipe is best when strawberries are at their peak season, usually during June. However, you can always make this recipe with marshmallows alone as they are always in season!

20 large marshmallows and/or ripe and juicy strawberries

1 cup Divvies Semisweet Chocolate Chips

20 mini paper baking cups (about 1¼ inches in diameter)

1. Cover a serving tray with baking cups.

2. If using strawberries, rinse them thoroughly to remove dirt and dust, and allow to dry completely. If there is any remaining moisture, the chocolate will not adhere well to the strawberry.

3. Melt the chocolate in the microwave or in a double boiler. (See tips on melting chocolate on page 41.)

4. Either hold each strawberry or marshmallow between your fingers or stick a toothpick into the end of each (at the stem end of the strawberries). Dip each strawberry or marshmallow into the melted chocolate allowing any excess to drip back into the bowl.

5. Once coated in chocolate, place each strawberry or marshmallow into a paper baking cup.

6. The strawberries and marshmallows can be served as soon as the chocolate has set, about 20 minutes. Store the dipped strawberries in the refrigerator for up to 24 hours. The marshmallows will keep in an airtight container for up to a week and do not have to be refrigerated.

Makes 20 marshmallows and/or strawberries

Snack Attack

We've all been there. You look up at the clock and it's 3:00 P.M.
You look out your window and see hungry kids tearing off the school bus,
making a beeline right to your kitchen before their playdate begins.
No need to panic! The ingredients you need to make delicious and
creative snacks are probably right in your pantry. And if they
are not, I am hoping these quick and easy recipes will inspire you
to stock up for these unexpected occasions! (For crowd-pleasing snacks,
trust me, chocolate is your friend—especially melted chocolate!)
These are my tried and trues.

For more information on working with melted chocolate, see page 41.

Individual Two-Minute Chocolate "Fondue"

All you really need to start this quick and simple recipe are Divvies Chocolate Chips, tiny ramekins, and toothpicks. This is such a fun and easy snack for sleepovers or after-school playdates.

Divvies Semisweet Chocolate Chips

SUGGESTED "FONDUE" DIPPERS:
Strawberries
Bananas
Cubes of vanilla cake
Pretzels
Marshmallows
Pineapple
Mini 5.5-ounce ramekins (one per guest)
Toothpicks (festive, themed ones if you are so inclined, such as American flags for the Fourth of July)

1. Prepare a platter of fruits, cake cubes, marshmallows, etc. by neatly displaying each item type in rows. Include either a serving utensil or toothpicks so guests can help themselves.

2. Put 1 cup of chocolate chips at a time into a microwave-safe bowl and place them in the microwave.

3. Depending on the power of your microwave, set the power level at medium or high for 2 minutes.

4. Remove the bowl from the microwave and stir the chocolate very well, so the heat from the melted chips can melt the unmelted chips. If all the chocolate hasn't melted after stirring, continue heating the chocolate in 15-second intervals in the microwave and stir again until all the chips are just melted and the chocolate is smooth. (Once the chocolate is melted, do not heat any longer, as it will burn.)

5. Pour the melted chocolate fondue into individual ramekins and serve immediately before it solidifies.

Mini Marshmallow Chocolate Clusters *Makes twenty-five clusters*

These chocolate candies take no time to make—and no time to eat! The thin, hardened chocolate shell around the soft marshmallow is a fantastic combination. This recipe has saved the day many times when I needed to quickly whip up a dessert to bring to a party.

2 cups Divvies Semisweet Chocolate Chips
1½ cups mini marshmallows
Mini paper baking cups

1. Melt 2 cups of chocolate chips in the microwave for 2 minutes, and stir to ensure that all the chocolate has melted. If all the chocolate hasn't melted, continue heating in 15-second intervals in the microwave, stirring until all the chips are melted and the chocolate is smooth.
2. Add 1½ cups of mini marshmallows to the melted chocolate and stir until the marshmallows are completely coated.
3. Spoon clusters of about six chocolate-covered marshmallows into mini paper baking cups.
4. Allow the chocolate to harden for about 30 minutes. Store in an airtight container.

Variation: For an extra-fun touch, add broken pretzel pieces and/or raisins to the bowl of melted chocolate when mixing.

Fun with Melted Chocolate

You can cover just about any of your favorite treats in chocolate!:

- Dried apricots or orange peels (follow instructions used for dipping strawberries and marshmallows on page 74)
- Potato chips
- Matzoh or cookies (dip in chocolate and allow to set for 20 minutes)
- Popcorn (spread in a single layer on a cookie sheet, drizzle liberally with chocolate, and allow to set for 20 minutes).

Flash-in-the-Pan S'mores *Makes six S'mores*

You don't need to rub sticks together to make this quick treat. It can all be done under the broiler. Be prepared to make a few trays of these—you'll be glad you did!

12 graham crackers (honey, plain, or other)
3 Divvies BingGo! Divvine Chocolate Bars, divided in half
6 large marshmallows

1. Preheat the oven to broil.
2. Break the graham crackers into 2½-inch squares and arrange six squares on a baking sheet so they are at least 1 inch apart.
3. Place 1 piece of chocolate on each graham cracker.
4. Put 1 large marshmallow on top of each piece of chocolate.
5. Place the baking sheet in the oven and *stay right there!* As soon as the marshmallows turn golden brown, take the baking sheet out of the oven. Put the other half of the graham cracker on top of each marshmallow and smush it down so that the marshmallow and chocolate melt together a little bit between the two crackers.
6. Have slightly damp napkins on hand for all those sticky fingers!

Twists on Chocolate

You can flavor your melted chocolate, too! Just add:

- Peppermint extract (mix in ¼ teaspoon per cup of chocolate)
- Orange zest or crushed peppermint pieces (2 tablespoons per cup of chocolate)

Blender Sundaes *Makes one 1¼-cup sundae*

Sundae bars are always a hit because each guest can concoct to their heart's content. I recommend you add ¼ cup of a mix-in for every cup of dairy-free "ice cream."

1 cup dairy-free ice cream, in assorted flavors

¼ CUP OF THE FOLLOWING MIX-INS:
Chocolate syrup
Mini marshmallows
Crumbled graham crackers
Chocolate chip cookie dough
Brownie batter
Crushed peppermint
Crushed favorite cereals
Sliced strawberries
Cherries
Sliced bananas

1. Place the dairy-free ice cream and mix-in of choice in a blender.
2. Blend until the mix-ins are evenly distributed throughout.
3. Using an ice-cream scoop, transfer sundaes into serving bowls.

Wafflewiches

I don't know about you, but I'm never without frozen waffles. So making these easy wafflewiches is as simple as heating the waffles and scooping dairy-free ice cream in between to make a 'wich.

Dairy-free ice cream (1 large scoop per wafflewich)
Frozen dairy-, nut-, egg-free waffles (we love the Belgian-style) (two per person)

1. Preheat the oven to 350 degrees. If you are making several wafflewiches, line a baking sheet with parchment paper or aluminum foil. (If you are making one or two, you can simply toast the waffles in the toaster.)
2. Place the waffles on the prepared baking sheet and bake in the preheated oven for 5 to 7 minutes, or until they are crisp and warm.
3. Let the waffles cool a bit to prevent the ice cream from melting. Press a scoop of dairy-free ice cream between the two waffles.

Variation: Make "ice cream" sandwiches with Benjamin's Chocolate Chip Cookies. Using two cookies per person press a scoop of dairy-free ice cream between the two cookies.

Summer Fruit Kabobs *Makes 10*

Delicious and nutritious on a stick! Kids who would never dive into a fruit salad will grab these nutritious, mouthwatering chunks of fruit—no utensils required. If you are in a rush, purchase pre-cut fruit from your local grocer as long as there is no chance of cross-contamination with allergens.

Fresh fruit of your choice:
1 cup cubed watermelon, cut into 1-inch dice
1 cup grapes
1 cup whole strawberries, stems removed
1 cup blueberries
1 cup raspberries
1 cup pineapple chunks, cut into 1-inch dice
1 cup cubed melon, cut into 1-inch dice
1 cup cherries, pitted
10 slices star fruit
10 bamboo barbecue skewers (about 10½ inches long)

1. Thread six to seven pieces of fruit on each bamboo skewer, alternating the fruit as you choose. Store the kabobs either in a plastic bag or covered in plastic wrap.

2. For easy handling, I usually put a few of the smallest fruits at the top ends, and leave room at the bottom of the skewer for all those anxious fingers. For a gorgeous party platter, I pile up the kebobs in one direction for easy grabbing, or fan them on a round platter.

Create Your Own Specialty "Ice Cream" Flavors

You don't need to buy multiple flavors of dairy-free ice cream, you can make them at home using the base flavor of your choice.

Simply place the base flavor (i.e. chocolate or vanilla) in a mixing bowl. Add fillings of your choice in the amount you desire, mix the ingredients together, and place in the freezer in an airtight container until ready to enjoy.

Some mix-in ideas:

Benjamin's Chocolate Chip Cookie dough (recipe on page 65)

Brownie batter (recipe on page 62)

Crushed peppermint

Freshly sliced strawberries

Divvies Semisweet Chocolate Chips

Dairy-free chocolate syrup

Mini marshmallows

"Brown" Chocolate Bag (p. 42)

Lemon Squares (p. 34)

Oh Fudge! (p. 39)

no nuts
no eggs
no dairy
(just delicious!)

Benjamin's
Chocolate Chip
Cookies

50 cents

bake
sale

75 cents

MADE
WITHOUT
PEANUTS
TREE NUTS
EGGS
MILK

It's Your Party!

Chocolate Cupcakes with "Cream Cheese" Frosting (p. 58 and p. 120); Chocolate Devil's Food Cake with Easy Icing (p. 128 and p. 131); Chocolate-Dipped Marshmallow Pops (p. 125); Squish Kabob Party Favors (p. 127)

Cinnamon Buns (p. 24)

Pick-Your-Berry Muffins (p. 88)

Warm Apple-Apricot Cake (p. 19)

OUTDOORS
AND
ON THE ROAD

From Vacation to Tailgate,

Picnic to Playdate

Destination Anywhere

Travel is important family time, and the stuff of which lifetime memories are made. So make sure your next vacation is fun, relaxed, and, of course, accompanied by great food! Over the years our family has done a lot of traveling. I've learned that there are many things you can do as a parent to lessen the anxiety of leaving the home base when your child has food allergies (even if you're just setting up a tent in the backyard for a night of stargazing!).

Ready, Set, Go . . .

Whether your travel plans call for flying domestically, internationally, or loading up the car for a short road trip, make sure you have packed some safe snacks and possibly even an easy-to-eat, protein-filled meal just in case. You never know when your flight might be delayed!

While we always call ahead to inform airlines and hotels about Benjamin's food allergies, it is still the first thing that we discreetly mention upon arrival. The idea is to take care of that business right away so we can get to the fun.

Always call ahead. If you are staying in a hotel, make sure your room has a refrigerator or arrange to have use of a refrigerator during your stay. If you are making restaurant reservations, be very specific about your family's food needs, and make sure they are understood. Stress that everyone's meals should be served at the same time. Remember to ask about the ingredients in any complimentary foods, such as breads.

Pack lots of food and drink—for everyone to share—for long car rides in case you cannot locate a restaurant that can accommodate your child.

If you are traveling internationally, have all the information concerning your family's food safety written in the language of the country you are visiting. It is a good idea to preplan your meals for the first day of the trip. This will eliminate a lot of the stress of figuring out where to eat when you first arrive at your destination. We include Benjamin in these plans so he can focus on having fun.

At the Ballgame

We find ourselves at big, crowded stadiums *a lot* because Benjamin loves the Mets and Jets! If you love your sports outings, too, follow these tips so you don't drop the ball on food safety.

- When tailgating, have aluminum foil on hand to avoid cross contamination when grilling.
- Bring lots of safe snacks to share with your group.
- If you plan to eat at the stadium, call ahead and speak to the catering manager so the food service can prepare meals and snacks safely to your specifications.
- Ask the catering manager to inform you which vendors at the concessions stands carry safe snacks.

Dining Out

Be expected! When you make dining reservations, try ordering the meal for your guest with food allergies so the restaurant kitchen and waitstaff are prepared for your arrival. Review your specific requests. Often extra time is necessary when making allergy-safe meals. This will help to have all diners' meals ready at the same time.

When Benjamin was younger, I would actually write out a schedule for the day and review it with him so he could think about where he was going to be and what he would eat.

Benjamin's Favorite Away-From-Home Snacks

Frozen chicken tenders

Frozen french fries

Pasta and sauce

Microwavable rice and soy sauce

Turkey sandwich

Cut up raw veggies

Beef jerky

Mini bags of pretzels and chips

Ice pops

Flavored gelatin

Apples, bananas, grapes

Dairy-free ice cream

Divvies cookies

Divvies Benjamint Crunch Bars

Divvies kettle corn

Fruit leathers

On a Playdate

Whether Benjamin is going on a playdate or packing for a sleepover, I always send along some of his favorite snacks. With the kids running around outside and keeping busy, it's best to have easy food options on hand. These items will quickly become staples in your friends' pantries!

Fruity Frozen Slushies

How's this for a home run? This dessert is not only refreshing, nutritious, and delicious; it also doubles as an ice pack, keeping everything else in your picnic basket cold. Make these the night before your outing so they are nice and frozen when you pack them in with your other food. When you arrive they will be the perfect slushy consistency.

1. Use packaged frozen fruit, or place fresh cherries, strawberries, and raspberries on a parchment-lined tray in freezer for at least 1 hour to freeze.
2. Place all ingredients (except watermelon) in a food processor, and process until all ingredients are slightly chunky.
3. Add watermelon and pulse until your desired consistency is achieved.
4. Pour the slushie mixture, to within 1 inch from the top, in small plastic containers that have covers. Do *not* cover now to allow for expansion in the freezer.
5. Freeze for at least 2 hours.
6. Cover with lids and pack with spoons or straws.

Makes 4 slushies

½ cup frozen cherries, pits removed

1 cup frozen strawberries

½ cup frozen raspberries

½ cup orange juice concentrate, thawed

2 tablespoons confectioners' sugar

1 cup fresh watermelon, seeds removed, cut into 1-inch cubes

Variation: Make slushies using other fruits, such as melons, bananas, and peaches. Be sure to use the same proportions of fruit stated in the recipe above.

Pick-Your-Berry Muffins

Summer is the best time to bake these, because every berry imaginable is at its peak. Plus, I love to get the kids involved in creating desserts (sometimes, though, I need to control their involvement so I am not in the kitchen forever and staring down a huge mess when we're done). For this recipe, I mix up the batter myself and pour it into the muffin tins. Then I line up the little green cardboard berry containers filled with strawberries, blueberries, raspberries, and blackberries, and let everyone pick their favorites. They simply drop the berries into the batter and voila! They've "made their own" muffins. These don't always make it into the picnic basket because the anticipation, coupled with the aroma, lands everyone around the oven when I take them out.

2 cups all-purpose flour

¾ teaspoon baking soda

½ teaspoon salt

1 cup sugar

1 cup soy milk

¼ cup canola oil

1 tablespoon white vinegar

1 cup berries such as strawberries, raspberries, blueberries, or a combination

Divvies Semisweet Chocolate Chips (optional)

1. Preheat the oven to 350 degrees.
2. Lightly coat 12-well muffin pan with nonstick baking spray.
3. Whisk the flour, baking soda, and salt in a medium mixing bowl. Set aside.
4. In a separate mixing bowl using an electric mixer, beat the sugar, soy milk, oil, and vinegar on medium speed.
5. Add the dry ingredients to the wet ingredients and beat well. Scrape down the sides of the bowl well, and continue beating.
6. Fill the muffin wells with batter, about two-thirds full. Distribute ½ cup of berries and/or chocolate chips evenly into each muffin and gently stir so they are enveloped with batter.
7. Bake the muffins for 23 to 28 minutes. Halfway through baking, divide the remaining ¼ cup of berries among the muffins and place a few on top of each.

8. When the muffin tops become lightly browned, insert a toothpick. When it comes out clean, the muffins are done.

9. Remove from the oven and allow to cool on a wire rack for 5 minutes. Gently invert the pan to release the muffins and continue cooling on the rack.

Makes 12 muffins

> *Go berry picking! What a great activity that everyone can do together. And, you've already planned the "what can we eat?" part of the adventure—berries!*

Freezing Berries Is Easy!

Keep your favorites in the freezer and avoid a trip to the market.

- Pick or purchase the freshest, ripest berries you can find.
- Gently rinse the berries, discarding damaged or overripe berries, stems, and leaves.
- Drain the berries using a colander, then place them on paper towels and blot them completely dry with more paper towels.
- Spread the clean, dry berries onto a baking sheet in a single layer.
- Place the baking sheet in the freezer overnight. This will allow the berries to freeze individually and not stick together when you bag them for storage.
- The next morning, remove the berries from the freezer. Place the berries into a freezer bag. Double-bag each package of berries to extend their storage life.

Corn Muffins

This is my favorite corn muffin, because they are a bit sweeter than most. If you prefer yours less so, cut the sugar to ½ cup. When I make the recipe with corn kernels (optional), I puree the corn because my kids don't care for whole kernels in their muffins.

1½ cups unbleached flour

¾ cup cornmeal (degerminated)

½ teaspoon baking powder

½ teaspoon salt

½ cup dairy-free margarine, softened

⅔ cup sugar

¼ cup honey or agave nectar

½ cup silken tofu, pureed

½ cup soy milk

OPTIONAL MIX-INS (¾ CUP OF ONE OF THE FOLLOWING)

Corn kernels

Blueberries (optional)

Canned crushed pineapple, strained

1. Preheat the oven to 400 degrees. Line a 12-well muffin pan with paper liners or spray with nonstick baking spray. (Or spray three 5 × 3-inch mini loaf pans with nonstick spray if you want to make cornbread.)

2. In a medium bowl, whisk together the flour, cornmeal, baking powder, and salt. Set aside.

3. In a mixing bowl, using an electric mixer cream together the margarine, sugar, honey or agave nectar, and tofu on medium speed. Be sure to scrape down the sides of the bowl with a spatula; the bowl will be slightly sticky from the honey.

4. Add the dry ingredients to the wet ingredients. Beat on medium speed. Scrape down the sides of the bowl and continue mixing on medium speed.

5. Add the milk and, if desired, fold in by hand the corn kernels and either whole or pureed blueberries or pineapple by pulsing in a food processor. Mix until evenly distributed throughout batter; do not overwork.

6. Spoon the batter into prepared muffin or loaf pans.

7. Bake the muffins for 25 to 30 minutes, rotating the pans and switching racks halfway through the baking time. When a toothpick inserted into the center of a muffin comes out clean, the muffins are done.

8. Remove from the oven and allow to cool on a wire rack for 5 minutes. Gently invert the pan to release the muffins from the pan and continue cooling on the rack.

Makes 12 muffins

Chocolate-Zucchini Bread

Here's a great way to get the kids to eat their zucchini! Chocolate lovers will appreciate the super-moistness and all the delicious chocolate chips in each slice. This recipe makes wonderful muffins as well.

1¼ cups thinly grated zucchini

1 cup unbleached flour

½ cup unsweetened cocoa powder

1 teaspoon baking soda

¼ teaspoon baking powder

¼ teaspoon salt

½ teaspoon ground cinnamon

½ cup canola oil

½ cup granulated sugar

½ cup packed light brown sugar

¼ cup applesauce

1 tablespoon white vinegar

1 teaspoon vanilla extract

1 cup Divvies Semisweet Chocolate Chips

1. Preheat the oven to 350 degrees. Spray a 9 × 5-inch loaf pan with nonstick baking spray.

2. Squeeze the grated zucchini over a colander to remove as much water as possible. Set aside.

3. Whisk the flour, cocoa powder, baking soda, baking powder, salt, and cinnamon in a medium bowl. Set aside.

4. In the bowl, using an electric mixer on medium speed, beat the oil, granulated and light brown sugars, applesauce, vinegar, and vanilla until well combined. Scrape down the sides of the bowl with a spatula and continue mixing.

5. Add the zucchini and mix in on low speed until well incorporated with the wet ingredients.

6. Add the flour mixture and beat on medium speed until just combined.

7. Add the chocolate chips and beat briefly on low speed until just combined.

8. Pour the batter into the prepared pan and bake in the preheated oven for 70 to 80 minutes. Insert a toothpick into the center of the loaf to test for doneness. The baking time will vary based on the moisture of the zucchini.

9. When done, remove the loaf from the oven, place on a wire rack, and let cool for at least 15 minutes. Then remove the loaf from the pan and cool completely.

Makes one 9 × 5-inch loaf; 10 slices

Prepare Zucchini in 4 Easy Steps

1. Choose a medium-size, shiny, and firm zucchini without visible cuts or scratches. Larger zucchini is tougher and contains more seeds.
2. Store unwashed zucchini in perforated plastic bags in the crisper drawer of the refrigerator. For best quality, use zucchini within four days.
3. Wash the zucchini just before use. There is no need to peel the zucchini if it is clean. Cut off the ends.
4. You may grate zucchini by hand or in a food processor. The zucchini should be finely grated, not pureed. You may need to cut the zucchini into smaller, more manageable pieces before grating or processing. Process in small batches to ensure proper consistency.

Chocolate Chip–Pumpkin Squares

This recipe was passed along from my friend Carolyn to my friend Andrea to me, and now I am happily passing it on to you. Of course "our" version is milk-, dairy-, and egg-free, and just as delicious as theirs!

2 cups flour

1 tablespoon ground pumpkin pie spice or ground apple pie spice

1 teaspoon baking soda

¾ teaspoon salt

1 cup dairy-free margarine

1¼ cups sugar

¼ cup applesauce

2 teaspoons vanilla extract

1 cup canned pumpkin puree

1 cup Divvies Semisweet Chocolate Chips

1. Preheat the oven to 350 degrees. Prepare a 9 × 9-inch or 13 × 9-inch pan by lining it with long pieces of aluminum foil. Extra foil should hang over the sides for easy lifting after baking.

2. Whisk the flour, pumpkin or apple pie spice, baking soda, and salt together in a medium bowl. Set aside.

3. Cream the margarine and sugar together in a bowl using an electric mixer on medium speed until smooth.

4. Add the applesauce, vanilla, and pumpkin puree and continue mixing on medium speed. Be sure to scrape down the sides of the bowl to incorporate all the ingredients, and continue mixing.

5. Combine the dry ingredients with the wet ingredients and mix on medium speed until just combined. Scrape down the sides of the bowl and continue mixing.

6. Add the chocolate chips and mix on low speed to distribute evenly throughout the batter.

7. Pour the batter into the prepared pan and bake for approximately 50 minutes. Insert a toothpick in the middle. If it comes out clean, the squares are done.

8. Cool the squares completely in the pan for at least 1 hour. Lift the aluminum foil out of the pan and cut into squares.

Makes sixteen or twenty-four 2-inch squares

Chocolate - Covered Monkey Pops

My son Max and I agree that this treat combines the best parts of a banana split on a stick! These are really easy to make and they travel well in an airtight container, packed in a cooler with ice. You can bring these along to picnics or for treats after a game.

1. Peel the bananas. Cut a small piece off one of the ends and insert one-third of the length of the popsicle stick vertically into the cut end of each banana.

2. Lay the bananas on a plate lined with parchment paper, and freeze for about 2 hours, or until they become very firm. Be sure to keep the bananas in the freezer until just before you are about to coat them in melted chocolate.

3. Pour the canola oil over the chocolate chips and melt. (See instructions for melting chocolate on page 41.)

4. Once the chocolate is melted, take the bananas out of the freezer. Using an icing spatula, and working quickly, spread the melted chocolate over each banana, coating very well. If desired, dip the coated bananas in sprinkles.

5. Since the bananas are frozen, the chocolate will firm up quickly. Store the bananas in an airtight container in the freezer until ready to serve.

Makes 6 pops

6 firm and ripe medium bananas

1½ cups Divvies Semisweet Chocolate Chips

1 tablespoon canola oil

Sprinkles

6 popsicle sticks

The IPie—Cherry or Blueberry or Apple

When it comes to food, mini usually means "mine," and kids love anything they can have to themselves! Use individual pie crusts from the baking section of the supermarket (read the ingredients carefully to be sure they are safe), or make your own crust from scratch (see recipe on page 98). If you're going to buy pie crust sheets, I find that the ones that come folded in a box are more pliable than those sold in the frozen section. These individual desserts are great for summer picnics because their small size makes them more travel-friendly than their larger counterparts. I've included instructions for three of our family's favorite fillings to get you started.

4 pie crust sheets

1/2 to 3/4 cup sugar, depending on tartness of cherries and your personal taste (you may want to increase sugar for cherry pie)

2 tablespoons flour

1/2 teaspoon ground cinnamon

4 1/4 cups fresh cherries, with stems removed and pitted, or blueberries, or apples (peeled, cored, and cut into 1/4-inch chunks)

1 teaspoon vanilla extract

2 tablespoons dairy-free margarine

1. Preheat the oven to 400 degrees. Spray two 5 1/2-inch mini pie plates with nonstick baking spray.

2. Remove the pie crusts from the box and gently unfold them onto lightly floured wax paper. Using a pie dish as a guide, cut two circles per IPie out of the store-bought pastry sheets, making them a bit wider than the widest diameter of the pie plate. This is for the top and bottom crusts.

3. Drape the crusts for the bottom of each pie evenly over each pie plate.

4. In a large bowl, whisk together the sugar, flour, and cinnamon.

5. Add the fruit and vanilla to the bowl with the sugar mixture, and using a large spoon, gently toss so the fruit is well coated.

6. Divide the mixture among the lined pie plates.

7. Cut the margarine into small pieces, and sprinkle equal amounts over the fruit mixture of each pie.

8. Place the second crust over the top of the fruit mixture in each pie plate. Fold the edges of the top crust

over and under the bottom edge of the bottom crust and pinch together.

9. Cut 5 to 6 small vent holes in the top crust of each pie.

10. Place on a baking sheet and bake in the preheated oven for 35 to 40 minutes, or until the top is golden brown and the fruit is bubbling up. If you notice the edges are starting to brown too fast, cover just the edges with a piece of aluminum foil to prevent burning.

11. Allow the pies to cool completely before serving.

Makes two 5½-inch pies

To avoid a potential mess when baking pies, line an oven rack with aluminum foil before placing the pie in the oven to catch any of the fruit juices that may bubble over the sides of the pie plate.

Basic Pie Crust

Are you a "make everything from scratch" kind of baker?
If so, you'll love this great all-purpose pie crust!

2 cups sifted flour

½ teaspoon salt

1 cup Crisco All-Vegetable Shortening

3 to 4 tablespoons cold water

1 tablespoon sugar for sprinkling on top of the pie

1. Mix together the flour and salt in a large bowl.
2. Add the shortening into the flour and salt mixture. Cut the shortening into the flour mixture; it should look like pea-size pieces.
3. Slowly add the water tablespoon by tablespoon and mix lightly with a fork until all of the flour is moistened and starts to come together in a ball.
4. Shape the mixture into a ball with your hands, flatten the ball, and wrap in wax paper or plastic wrap. Refrigerate overnight, or from morning to evening.
5. Spray two 9-inch pie dishes or four 5½-inch mini pie dishes with nonstick baking spray (made with flour).
6. Remove the dough from the refrigerator and remold into a ball.
7. Cut the ball in half and roll each half into a smaller ball.
8. Tear off two sheets of wax paper and sprinkle and spread flour over one piece.
9. Place one dough ball on the wax paper and sprinkle flour on top of the dough.
10. Put the second sheet of wax paper on top and then roll the dough out with a rolling pin, until it is very thin and large enough to fit your pie pan.
11. Remove the top sheet of wax paper, flip the dough over, and then press into the pie pan. Gently peel off the other piece of wax paper.

12. Sprinkle a little flour on the bottom crust, which will help to absorb liquid from the fruit filling.

For the Upper Crust

1. Preheat the oven to 425 degrees.
2. Roll out the other half of the pie dough, following directions above, and place carefully on top of the pie filling.
3. Peel off the wax paper.
4. Use the tines of a fork to make about 8 to 10 fork holes on top of each pie, or put three slits with a sharp knife across top crusts before baking. Use the fork (or your fingers) to press the two layers of dough together all around the edge of the pie dish.
5. Sprinkle sugar on top of the pie.
6. Bake according to pie recipe instructions.

Makes two 9-inch pie crusts

Cinnamon-Sugary Oatmeal Crumb Topping

For the ultimate in comfort food, make this crumb topping for your pies!

½ cup flour

½ cup old-fashioned oats (not instant)

½ cup packed light brown sugar

½ cup packed dark brown sugar

½ teaspoon ground cinnamon
½ cup chilled dairy-free margarine

1. Whisk together the flour, oats, sugars, and cinnamon in a mixing bowl. Set aside.
2. Cut margarine into ¼-inch pieces and scatter over the dry ingredients.
3. Using an electric mixer, beat the flour mixture and margarine at low speed until they resemble crumbs.
4. Sprinkle the crumb topping over the filled pie crust, and bake the pie according to recipe instructions.

Makes 2 cups crumb topping

Quickest Pie Ever!

You can also find ready-made graham cracker crusts in the baking section of your market. For the quickest pie-making experience, fill the ready-made crusts with canned pie filling, top with crumb topping, and bake at 400 degrees for 30 minutes.

Strawberry-Rhubarb Free-form Tarts

Growing up, my family used to enjoy homemade pies sold at a local farmstand. My brother David's favorite was always the strawberry-rhubarb pie, and that is what inspired the flavor of this tart. Like the IPie (page 96), this recipe can be made into four individual tarts so everyone can have their own.

1. Put the flour, salt, and sugar in a food processor and pulse for 15 seconds to combine. Add the margarine and pulse for another 15 seconds. Pour half of the ice water through the feed tube very slowly with the food processor running. Turn off the food processor, and test the dough by pinching it with your fingers. It should just hold together, and not feel dry and crumbly. If necessary, add the remaining water and continue to process for 15 to 20 seconds. Do not overprocess.

2. Divide and form dough into two to four even balls. Wrap with plastic wrap, and refrigerate for 45 minutes.

3. Prepare a baking sheet by lining it with parchment paper and set aside.

4. To make the filling, combine the rhubarb, strawberries, sugar, flour, and strawberry-rhubarb preserves in a large bowl. Set aside.

5. Lightly flour a flat, clean, dry surface or board and roll out each portion of dough into a circle about 7 inches in diameter if you are making four tarts, and slightly larger, about 9 inches, if you are making two larger tarts.

6. Preheat the oven to 400 degrees.

THE CRUST

1¼ cups unbleached flour

½ teaspoon salt

1 tablespoon sugar

½ cup dairy-free margarine, chilled and cut into 1-inch pieces

¼ cup ice water

THE FILLING

1½ cups rhubarb, cut into ½-inch pieces (see variation)

1½ cups strawberries, cut into ½-inch pieces

½ cup sugar

¼ cup unbleached flour

¼ cup strawberry-rhubarb preserves

7. Evenly divide the filling among the crusts. Spoon filling into the middle of each crust leaving a 1½-inch border, uncovered, around the outside edges.

8. Gently fold the edges of the crust up and over the filling. Do not cover the center of the tarts.

9. Return the assembled tarts, covered in plastic wrap, to the refrigerator for about 15 minutes to chill.

10. Bake the tarts in the preheated oven for approximately 25 minutes, or until the crust is golden and fruit juices start bubbling and running out of the center of the tart.

11. Cool the tarts on a wire rack before serving.

Makes four 5½-inch tarts or two larger tarts

Variation: Since rhubarb may not be available at your grocer throughout the year, you can substitute 1½ cups of Granny Smith apples and 2 tablespoons of lemon juice. This will replace the rhubarb's crunchy texture and tart taste very nicely.

Trail Mix Buffet

With the endless types of trail mix at your grocery store, it's clear that everyone prefers a different variation—especially kids. So let them make their own, knowing it's healthy, safe, and totally customized. Put all the ingredients in little bowls, buffet style, and distribute reusable containers to each child so they can concoct their own mix.

1. Combine the desired ingredients in the proportions you like.
2. If not packing in individual bags right away, store the trail mix in an airtight container in a cool, dry place. The mix will usually keep for up to 2 months.

Makes 1 cup per person

Keep trail mix in clear containers or Mason jars with a small scoop on your kitchen counter. Encourage everyone to scoop some for themselves to eat alone or mixed in with cereal, dairy-free "ice cream," oatmeal, etc.

SUGGESTED MIXABLES

1 cup dried cranberries

1 cup dried pineapple

1 cup dried blueberries

1 cup dried apple

1 cup sunflower seeds

1 cup mini marshmallows

1 cup Divvies Semisweet Chocolate Chips

1 cup cereal of your choice

1 cup currants

1 cup dried cherries

1 cup pumpkin seeds

1 cup mini pretzels

1 cup crystallized ginger

1 cup banana chips

1 cup oat squares cereal

1 cup soy nuts

1 cup dried date pieces

Andrea's Mom's Granola Bars

Food triggers so many childhood memories, and for many bakers like myself, our favorite recipes, written on little cards and kept in tiny tin boxes, are cherished keepsakes. Andrea's Mom's Granola is one such treasured recipe that has inspired me to concoct these granola bars. You definitely need to make these bars! They keep really well and make great snacks for the road.

4 cups oats

2 cups shredded wheat, torn by hand into threads, not dust!

2 cups puffed wheat or puffed rice

½ cup packed light brown sugar

¼ teaspoon salt

I cup honey or agave nectar

¾ cup nondairy margarine

½ to ¾ cup dried fruit of your choice

¼ cup sunflower or soy nut butter

½ cup Divvies Semisweet Chocolate Chips

1. Preheat the oven to 350 degrees.
2. Line two baking sheets with parchment paper.
3. Combine the oats, shredded wheat or puffed rice, brown sugar, and salt in a large mixing bowl. Transfer the mixture onto the two lined baking sheets.
4. Bake the granola for at least 20 minutes, stirring occasionally and watching carefully so it does not burn. Rotate the pans on the racks for even heat distribution. Remove the granola from the oven when caramel in color.
5. While the granola is baking, pour the honey or agave nectar into a small saucepan, and place over medium heat for 1 to 2 minutes until boiling. Turn off the heat.
6. Add the margarine to the honey and stir until completely melted.
7. Once the granola has baked, pour it into a large metal bowl and add the dried fruit. Keep the oven on.
8. Slowly pour the hot honey mixture over the granola. Mix with a spoon (that has been sprayed with nonstick cooking spray) until well coated.

9. Add the sunflower or soy nut butter, and mix with the coated spoon until the hot ingredients melt the sunflower seed butter.

10. Pour all the ingredients back onto one of the parchment-lined baking sheets. Place a fresh piece of parchment paper on top of the warm granola bar mixture, then lightly press the mixture with the heel of your hand, pressing it into a 12×6-inch rectangle.

11. Remove the top layer of parchment paper, and place the baking sheet back in the oven. Bake for 20 minutes, rotating the baking sheet twice.

12. Remove the granola bars from the oven and gently press chocolate chips evenly into the top. Let sit for 15 minutes, then cut into thirty-six 3×2-inch bars while still partially warm.

Makes 3 dozen 2 × 1-inch granola bars

Andrea's Mom's Granola tastes great as a topping on dairy-free "ice cream," on its own as a cereal, or mixed into oatmeal.

Suggested Dried Fruits

Dried cherries

Dried blueberries

Dried apricots

Dried apples

Dried raisins

Extra-Thick, Treasure-Filled Marshmallow Treats

It's hard to improve on these time-honored treats, and they're also hard to mess up, so go ahead and add the unexpected. My kids and their friends love that I cut these into 3-inch squares, individually wrap each one, and put them in a basket on top of the kitchen counter. This makes for an easy grab-and-go snack.

10 cups Rice Krispies cereal, or similar crisped rice cereal

2 cups Froot Loops cereal (or similar type) or 2 cups miniature marshmallows

6 tablespoons dairy-free margarine

9 cups miniature marshmallows

For a guilt-free spin on traditional marshmallow treats, use Fiber One cereal instead of Rice Krispies and Froot Loops.

---

1. Line a $13 \times 9 \times 2$-inch baking pan with a long piece of aluminum foil that extends over the edges of the pan. Spray the foil with nonstick cooking spray.

2. Mix the cereals together in a large pot sprayed with nonstick cooking spray.

3. In another large pot sprayed with nonstick cooking spray, slowly melt the margarine over medium heat.

4. Add nine cups of marshmallows to margarine and stir until just melted.

5. Remove the pot from the heat and pour the melted marshmallows over the cereal and/or marshmallow mixture, stirring with a large spoon coated with cooking spray.

6. Pour and spread the mixture into the prepared pan. Cover the mixture with a sheet of wax paper, and press extra hard with the heels of your hands, to evenly distribute the mixture in the pan—you really want these treats to be dense.

7. Cool for 20 minutes. Cut into eighteen 3×3-inch pieces. Remove the squares from the pan by lifting sides of foil. Wrap each square neatly with plastic

wrap so they will last longer and are ready to grab when you or the kids are on the run.

Makes 1 dozen 3 × 3-inch crispy marshmallow treats

Variation: With a large spoon and clean hands, mold finished mixture into 2-inch balls, and lightly press each ball into a flat-bottomed wafer cone. Voila! A fun twist on the everyday marshmallow treat.

Extra-large pots work best for this recipe.
To make absolutely perfect-looking marshmallow treats, cut them with an electric carving knife.

Vanilla Cookies

These cookies are so simple and delicious that you can use them as a base for any variety of cookies. My husband loves turning them into snickerdoodles. Max enjoys them with a refreshing lime icing. Benjamin and Adam love them plain.

3¼ cups all-purpose flour

1 teaspoon baking soda

1 teaspoon baking powder

½ teaspoon salt

¾ cup dairy-free margarine, at room temperature

2 cups sugar

1½ teaspoons Ener-G Egg Replacer

2 tablespoons water

1 tablespoon vanilla extract

1 cup Tofutti Better Than Sour Cream

To make snickerdoodles, mix 2 tablespoons of white sugar with 2 teaspoons of cinnamon in a small bowl. Roll scoops of cookie dough into the mixture, then drop onto the prepared baking sheet 2 inches apart and bake as directed above.

1. Preheat the oven to 375 degrees. Line three baking sheets with parchment paper.

2. In a medium bowl, whisk together the flour, baking soda, baking powder, and salt. Set aside.

3. Cream the margarine and sugar in a bowl with an electric mixer set on high speed until very smooth.

4. In a small bowl, beat the egg replacer and water by hand, using a whisk. Add dissolved egg replacer (be sure to add every drop) and the vanilla to the margarine and sugar mixture, and beat on medium speed. Scrape down the sides of the bowl with a spatula, and mix again.

5. Add the "sour cream," and mix until well combined.

6. Add the flour mixture to the wet ingredients, and mix on medium speed, scraping down the sides of the bowl and mixing again until well incorporated.

7. Scoop the cookies with a #40 cookie scoop, and drop onto the prepared baking sheets 2 inches apart.

8. Bake for 20 to 22 minutes, or until the cookies begin to turn golden brown on the edges.

9. Cool the cookies on the baking sheets for 10 minutes, then transfer to wire cooling racks.

10. If you desire, spread Key Lime Icing (page 109) on tops of cookies.

Makes 4 dozen 1½-inch cookies

Key Lime Icing

1. Stir together the sugar and key lime juice, by hand with a spoon or whisk, until the sugar has dissolved and the icing is smooth. Add a tiny amount of food coloring to the icing, and stir until the desired color is achieved.

2. Spread icing on tops of Vanilla Cookies (page 108) or other cookie of your choosing.

Makes 1 cup icing

1 cup confectioners' sugar

2 tablespoons key lime juice

Food coloring (optional)

Chocolate Toffee

Decadent dark chocolate over toffee, cut into irresistible bite-size pieces.
This is a great holiday gift, party favor, dessert, or well-deserved treat for yourself.

1¼ cups unsalted dairy-free margarine

1 cup granulated sugar

¼ cup firmly packed light brown sugar

¼ cup water

1 tablespoon dark molasses

½ teaspoon ground cinnamon

1 cup Divvies Semisweet Chocolate Chips

EQUIPMENT
candy thermometer

1. Line baking sheet with parchment paper. Set aside.
2. Melt margarine in a medium-size saucepan over low heat. Add the granulated sugar, brown sugar, water, and molasses and stir until the sugar dissolves.
3. Raise heat to medium and clip a candy thermometer onto the side of the pan. Stir the toffee mixture slowly and constantly until the thermometer registers 290 degrees. This should take about 15 minutes.
4. Wait an additional minute after the thermometer registers 290 degrees before removing the saucepan from heat (or else the toffee will end up crumbly). Add the cinnamon and stir until fully dissolved.
5. Pour the entire mixture onto the parchment-lined baking sheet immediately. Do not use toffee that sticks to the bottom of the saucepan.
6. Allow the toffee to cool for about 1 minute, and then sprinkle the chocolate chips over the toffee. Let stand for 1 minute to soften, and then spread the chocolate over the surface of the toffee using the back of a metal spoon (a soup spoon works best) until melted.
7. Refrigerate uncovered until the candy is firm, about 1 hour. Break into 2-inch pieces and store in an airtight container.

Makes 1 pound of 2-inch toffee pieces.

Chocolate Marshmallow Banana Boats

A blast from the past for all who remember their scouting campfire days.
Kids have tons of fun making this simple, scrumptious, ooey-gooey treat.

4 bananas (unpeeled)

1 cup mini marshmallows

1 cup Divvies Semisweet
Chocolate Chips

1. With the peel on, use a sharp paring knife to slice the bananas lengthwise. Be careful not to slice through the bottom skin. Using your fingers, gently open the slit so the banana will be similar in shape to a canoe. Place the marshmallows and chocolate chips inside the opening of the bananas.

2. Loosely wrap the bananas with aluminum foil and set directly on a barbeque grill or on the hot coals of a campfire for 15 minutes.

3. Using metal tongs, remove foil-wrapped bananas from the heat source. You can enjoy them right out of the foil (be careful—the foil will be hot!). Serve with a spoon.

Makes 4 banana boats

> *For easier serving and cleanup, place unwrapped banana boats in a disposable foil pan, cover with foil, and bake in a 400 degree oven for 20 minutes.*

Variations: Add Chocolate Toffee pieces (recipe, page 110) to the banana boats.

Place a banana boat in a bowl and add a scoop of dairy-free vanilla "ice-cream"—a fun twist on a banana split!

Cookie S'mores

. . . .

With all the melty, delicious layers in this dessert, you might call it the Club Sandwich of sweets. And at the Sandler house, we always seem to find s'more layers to add, like a layer of banana on top of the chocolate, which is on top of the marshmallow—yum! I like to substitute chocolate chip cookies for the traditional graham crackers, but that's up to you. I find the cookie adds lots of flavor to the stack and holds the "sandwich" together just like the traditional graham cracker.

1 marshmallow

½ piece of a Divvies BingGo! Divvine Chocolate bar

2 Benjamin's Chocolate Chip Cookies (page 65) per s'more (or if you are a traditionalist, 2 graham crackers)

2 thinly sliced pieces of banana (optional)

1. Roast the marshmallow by pressing it into the sharp end of a stick and holding it over an open fire, or by broiling it in the oven. Watch the marshmallow carefully, and remove it from the heat as soon as it becomes golden brown. For instructions on how to broil marshmallows, refer to Flash-in-the-Pan S'mores (page 78).

2. Place the piece of chocolate on top of the cookie.

3. If you love chocolate and bananas as much as my son, Max, place two slices of banana side by side on top of the chocolate.

4. Place the roasted marshmallow on top of the chocolate or bananas.

5. Place the second cookie on top of the marshmallow and gently press so the heat of the marshmallow lightly melts the chocolate. Wait 5 seconds before eating these so that you don't burn the roof of your mouth!

Makes 1 S'more per person

IT'S YOUR PARTY!

Celebrate with Sweets

that Everyone Can Eat

Party EtiTiquette

Birthdays are the perfect time to share friendship, fun, and food. So, keep things simple to ensure that everyone can enjoy the party. When the party is at your home serve the food treats that everyone not only wants to eat but *can* eat. There is absolutely no reason for anyone to feel left out at a birthday party (traditionally a smorgasbord of dairy-driven treats), especially when there are so many delectable and safe confections that are incredibly easy to make.

But what about *the party that is not at your house?* Don't panic but don't just send your child with a present, a defrosted cupcake, and a hope for the best. Take that donkey by his pinned-on tail and call the hostess as soon as your child receives the invitation to the party. You want to make sure you give your child's host plenty of time to comfortably work out food solutions. And, when you make that call, don't just rattle off your child's don't-touch food list and then expect the person on the other end of the phone to deal gracefully with the sudden dearth of menu options. Instead, tell her about your child's specific allergies and restrictions and then jump in with suggestions of what you could do to make her life easier and her party a huge success.

Ask the hostess what food will be served at the party, and tell her what you can make. Just bring it, that way the hostess does not feel guilty having to take you up on an offer. Make sure that the dessert you bring not only tastes great but looks festive, serving platter included.

If the party is a sleepover, find out what is being served for dinner and breakfast. Point out all the things on the menu that are safe for your child and then provide a few safe items that most kids love but she may not have

thought to include. Again, make sure you grab on to some of the items on her menu, and tell her you'll make and/or bring them. If dinner is a cookout with burgers and dogs, then why not bring "safe" hamburger and hotdog buns? Rise and shine in the eyes of your child's hosts by bringing breakfast treats the next morning for overtired tent-dwellers. Make Divvies Scones or Breakfast Cookies (pages 45 and 71) that kids love, and that have been known to bring parents to their knees in gratitude.

Vanilla Layer Cake

This cake is a huge hit with my kids and almost never makes it as a two-layer cake because they always eat the first layer before it cools. You can really have fun with this one, so I've offered a few ways you can reinvent this cake for various occasions. Remember to use cake flour for this recipe—it really makes a difference.

2½ cups cake flour

2½ tablespoons baking powder

½ teaspoon salt

1½ teaspoons Ener-G Egg Replacer

2 tablespoons unflavored seltzer

½ cup dairy-free margarine, softened at room temperature

1¼ cups sugar

1½ teaspoons vanilla extract

½ cup plus 2 tablespoons soy milk

1. Preheat the oven to 350 degrees. Generously spray two 9-inch round cake pans with nonstick baking spray.

2. Whisk the cake flour, baking powder, and salt. Set aside.

3. Emulsify the egg replacer and seltzer with a small whisk in a small bowl until frothy. Set aside.

4. In a large bowl, using an electric mixer, beat the softened margarine, sugar, vanilla, and egg replacer on high speed until fluffy. At least twice during mixing, scrape the sides and bottom of the bowl thoroughly in order to fully incorporate all the ingredients.

5. Add the flour mixture and soy milk to the sugar mixture alternately ¼ cup at a time. Mix on medium speed, scraping the sides and bottom of the bowl, until just incorporated; the batter will be stiff. Do not overmix.

6. Distribute and spread the batter evenly into the prepared cake pans.

7. Bake 24 to 28 minutes. The cakes are fully baked when a toothpick inserted in the middle comes out clean.

8. Cool the cake layers for 15 minutes before removing

from the pans and transferring to wire cooling racks. Cool completely before frosting or adding fillings.

Makes one 19-inch round 2-layer cake; 10 slices

Variations: Add alternate layers of fruit such as strawberries, blueberries, raspberries, or bananas between the layers. I like to mix the berries with a teaspoon of white sugar first, to bring out their juiciness and sweetness.

Spread chocolate pudding between the layers. You don't have to make homemade chocolate pudding, just buy pre-made soy pudding or make it from a packet. When I do this, I don't frost the sides of the cake, so everyone can see the pudding.

The delicious Raspberry Cream Frosting (page 119) tastes fantastic on this simple vanilla cake. You'll need to double the recipe if you're using the frosting in between the layers as well as on the outside of the cake.

Birthday Cake in a Cone

What's better than ice cream cones and cupcakes? Ice cream cone cupcakes!

1 recipe Vanilla Layer Cake batter (page 116)

1 cup Divvies Semisweet Chocolate Chips

1½ teaspoons flour

20 flat-bottomed wafer ice cream cones

Vanilla Frosting (page 61)

Sprinkles (optional)

1. Preheat the oven to 350 degrees.
2. Make the cake batter as directed.
3. In a small bowl, stir together the chocolate chips and flour. Stir the chip mixture into the cake batter.
4. Place each ice cream cone upright in muffin cups. Fill each cone half-full with batter.
5. Bake the filled cones 21 to 25 minutes, until a toothpick inserted in the center comes out clean.
6. While the cakes are baking, make the frosting. When the cakes are done, remove from the oven and cool completely. Frost and sprinkle!

Makes twenty cones

Sparklers aren't just for the Fourth of July. Use them to replace traditional birthday candles.

Raspberry Cream Frosting

This makes a really nice-tasting frosting. When purchasing seedless jam for this recipe, consider a variety that is a brighter red color for a prettier result.

1. Beat the margarine in a medium bowl with an electric mixer on medium speed until smooth. Slowly add the sugar while beating, until well incorporated.

2. In a microwave-safe bowl, whisk together the raspberry jam, cornstarch, and vanilla. Microwave on high for 1 to 1½ minutes, stopping once to mix, and stop the microwave when the mixture just starts to bubble. Carefully and quickly remove the bowl from the microwave and pour into a small mixing bowl. With a spoon, mix by hand. Place the bowl in the refrigerator for 8 to 10 minutes until it cools to room temperature.

3. Once at room temperature, add the thickened raspberry jam mixture to the creamed margarine and sugar. Beat on medium speed until well combined, smooth, and even in color.

4. Spread the frosting liberally on cakes and cupcakes.

Makes 3 cups frosting

2 cups dairy-free margarine

1⅓ cups confectioners' sugar

1 cup seedless raspberry jam (bright in color)

½ cup cornstarch (or substitute ½ cup confectioners' sugar if you want a very sweet frosting)

1 teaspoon vanilla extract

If you are frosting the outside of a cake in addition to between the layers of the cake, double this recipe.

Carrot Cake with "Cream Cheese" Frosting

Some prefer chocolate, some prefer vanilla—and then there are those who request "carrot" for their birthday cake! This recipe makes a moist, light sheet cake and lip-smacking frosting that you can divvy up into smaller squares. You'll be craving it throughout the day!

THE CAKE

3 cups all-purpose flour

1½ teaspoons baking powder

1 teaspoon baking soda

1½ teaspoons ground cinnamon

½ teaspoon ground nutmeg

¼ teaspoon ground cloves

½ teaspoon salt

8 peeled carrots

1½ cups granulated sugar

½ cup packed dark brown sugar

2 cups applesauce

1½ cups canola oil

1 cup currants or raisins (optional) or 1 cup Divvies Semisweet Chocolate Chips

For the Cake

1. Preheat the oven to 350 degrees. Spray a 13 × 9-inch baking pan with nonstick baking spray.

2. Whisk the flour, baking powder, baking soda, cinnamon, nutmeg, cloves, and salt in a large mixing bowl. Set aside.

3. Shred the carrots in a food processor using the shredding blade. Place the carrots on top of the combined dry ingredients. Do *not* mix together.

4. Wipe out the food processor bowl with paper towels and add the metal blade.

5. Process, in the food processor, the granulated and dark brown sugars, applesauce, and canola oil until well combined.

6. Pour the sugar mixture into a mixing bowl. Add carrots and dry ingredients and, using an electric mixer, mix on medium speed. If desired, add currants, raisins, or chocolate chips to the batter and mix on low speed to distribute evenly throughout. Scrape down the sides of the bowl with a spatula, and continue mixing until all the ingredients are well combined.

7. Pour the batter into the prepared pan. Bake for 45 to 50 minutes, rotating the pan halfway through the baking time. (If you found the carrots to be "watery" when shredded, extra baking time may be required.)

Test by inserting a toothpick in the middle to make sure the cake is done.

8. Cool the cake in the baking pan. Cooled cake may be removed from or left in the baking pan.

9. Frost with "cream cheese" frosting, if desired.

For the Frosting

1. In a bowl, and using an electric mixer, beat the margarine, "cream cheese," vanilla, and lemon extract on medium speed until well combined.

2. Slowly add the confectioners' sugar. Mix until smooth and creamy.

3. Store the frosting, covered, in the refrigerator, until ready to spread on the cooled cake.

Makes twenty-four 2-inch squares

THE FROSTING

1/2 cup dairy-free margarine, at room temperature

1/2 cup Tofutti Better Than Cream Cheese, at room temperature

1 1/2 teaspoons vanilla extract

1 teaspoon lemon extract

4 cups confectioners' sugar

This frosting also tastes delicious on the Chocolate Chip Pumpkin Squares (page 94).

"Ice Cream" and Sorbet Cake

Ice cream cake is a rare treat when dairy is not a part of your diet. Use your imagination to make this cake exactly as the birthday boy or girl wishes!

3 cups dairy-free vanilla "ice cream"

1 layer of Vanilla Layer Cake (page 116; for just 1 layer, make half of recipe)

4 cups raspberry sorbet

1 pint berries, such as raspberries or strawberries

¼ cup sugar

1. Allow the dairy-free ice cream to soften at room temperature for 20 minutes.

2. Trace and cut out a 9-inch circle of parchment paper and fit it into the bottom of a 9-inch springform pan. Cut out a 3 × 27-inch strip of parchment paper and fit it around the inside rim of the pan. Tape the parchment paper together where the ends overlap.

3. Cover the parchment paper-lined bottom of the pan with the layer of cake and spread the softened ice cream evenly over the cake. Freeze until the ice cream hardens, about 20 minutes.

4. While the ice cream is refreezing, take the sorbet out of the freezer and let soften at room temperature for 20 minutes.

5. Combine the berries and sugar. Remove the cake pan from the freezer and place the berries evenly over the ice cream. Return to the freezer for 5 minutes.

6. After 5 minutes remove the cake pan from the freezer and spread 2 cups of the softened sorbet over the berry layer.

7. Wrap the cake with plastic wrap and freeze for about 4 hours before serving.

8. When ready to serve, open the springform pan and remove the side layer of parchment. Use a large spatula to remove the cake from the bottom of the pan and

place the cake on a platter. Let it sit for 5 minutes to thaw just a bit. Cut into slices using a very sharp knife that has been dipped in warm water and wiped with a clean towel between slices.

Makes one 9-inch frozen cake; 10 slices

"Ice Cream" Hash

Cancel the clown! Making your own "Ice Cream" Hash is birthday entertainment at its best. Have a bowl or cup ready with each child's name written on it. The kids can create their own personalized "ice cream" flavor! Just make sure that all of the mix-in ingredients are safe for your attendees, and that surfaces are completely clean in order to avoid any chances for cross-contamination.

3 pints dairy-free "ice cream"

MIX-INS

Chocolate chips

Mini marshmallows

Cookie dough

Brownie batter

Crushed pineapple

Crushed graham crackers

Gummy bears

Cake bits

Brownie bits

Crushed Oreo cookies

Sprinkles

Crushed peppermint candies

Chocolate

Frozen, sweetened berries, thawed

Bananas

Cherries

1. Chill several large metal mixing bowls in your freezer. If you have a granite (or other nonporous stone) countertop that stays fairly cold, you can work directly on that instead of in a bowl.

2. Take the "ice cream" out of the freezer for 10 minutes and allow to soften at room temperature.

3. With a large spoon in each hand, flatten out scoops of softened ice cream in a chilled mixing bowl or on the countertop. Make the ice cream just flat enough so you can spread your mix-ins on top. Add the toppings and mix and mush together into the ice cream. The ratio should be 4:1 ice cream to mix-ins.

4. Scoop the ice cream hash into a bowl or cone and enjoy!

Makes six 1- to 2-cup "ice cream" hash servings

Chocolate-Dipped Marshmallow Pops

These pops look so cute when standing, with the marshmallow side sticking up, in a small glass filled with jelly beans or sprinkles.

1. Line a cookie sheet with wax paper or mini cupcake liners.
2. Press a lollipop stick into each marshmallow.
3. If decorating, set up an assembly line of the sprinkles, crushed peppermint, etc. in small bowls.
4. Microwave the chocolate and oil in a microwave-safe bowl on high for 2 minutes.
5. Stir to make sure all the melted chips melt the unmelted ones. Only if necessary (you do not want to burn the chocolate), microwave in additional 15-second intervals until all the chocolate has melted.
6. Hold the end of the lollipop stick and dip the marshmallows one at a time into the melted chocolate, allowing excess chocolate to drip back into the bowl.
7. If desired, immediately decorate by dipping the chocolate-covered marshmallow pops into the decorations.
8. Place the pops on wax paper or into mini cupcake liners and let stand to dry at room temperature.

Makes 30 pops

30 lollipop sticks (sold in the baking section of craft supply shops)

One 10.5-ounce package large marshmallows

2 cups Divvies Semisweet Chocolate Chips

1 tablespoon canola oil

DECORATIONS (OPTIONAL)

Sprinkles

Colored sugars

Nonpareils

Crushed peppermint hard candies

Movie Night Popcorn

Many Divvies customers order our gourmet popcorn to serve at birthday, slumber, and movie parties! It's made fresh to order at our bakery, and packaged in a huge circus-themed box along with a scoop and individual bags. Since popcorn made at movie theaters sometimes comes into contact with dairy through the melted butter topping, we've always made ours at home and taken it along. Divvies kernels pop up bigger and fluffier than most.

¼ cup olive oil

¾ cup Divvies gourmet popcorn kernels

1 tablespoon kosher salt

Canola, corn, or vegetable oil may be used in place of olive oil if you prefer.

1. Have some oven mitts ready. Use a 4-quart saucepan, big enough to hold the amount of popcorn you want to make. Pour olive oil to cover the entire bottom of the pot, about ⅛-inch deep. Place the pot on the stovetop over medium-high heat and preheat oil for about 30 seconds.

2. Add a single layer of kernels to cover the entire bottom of the pot, and cover the pot. The popcorn should start popping in about a minute.

3. Continuously shake the pot across the burner until the popping reaches a crescendo. Once the popping sounds subside significantly, and *before* they stop entirely, remove the pot from the burner. You may still hear intermittent popping.

4. Pour the popcorn into a large bowl(s), and sprinkle with salt to taste.

Makes 4 cups popcorn

Variation: Add any of the following mix-ins for variations on a movie popcorn theme. Use canola oil in the pot instead of olive oil if you're using sweet mix-ins. And if you want to make the experience extra-fun, do what we do at Divvies—give everyone their own personal bag!

Cinnamon candy

Pretzels

Raisins

Cherry licorice bits

Mini marshmallows

Graham cereal pieces

Corn chips

Rice crackers

Banana chips

Cocoa powder

Sugar

Cinnamon

Oregano

Red pepper flakes

Chili powder

Chocolate Devil's Food Cake

This cake is moist, rich, and chocolaty—and it looks great with fresh berries, including leaves and stems, and fresh mint leaves as a garnish. For a more decadent dessert, drizzle the cake with Dark Chocolate Glaze (page 130) or Easy Icing (page 131).

1 tablespoon white vinegar

1 cup soy milk

2 cups all-purpose flour

2 cups granulated sugar

¾ cup cocoa powder

2 teaspoons baking soda

½ teaspoon salt

3 teaspoons Ener-G Egg Replacer

4 tablespoons seltzer

1 cup Divvies Semisweet Chocolate Chips

1 cup boiling water

1 cup canola oil

½ teaspoon vanilla extract

1. Preheat the oven to 300 degrees. If you have one, set the oven to convection. Spray a bundt pan with non-stick baking spray and set aside.

2. Pour vinegar into the cup of soy milk (the vinegar will thicken the soy milk a bit) and set aside while you prepare the rest of the recipe.

3. Whisk together the flour, sugar, cocoa, baking soda, and salt and set aside.

4. Whisk together the egg replacer and seltzer until fully dissolved and frothy. Set aside.

5. Pour the chocolate chips into the bowl of an electric mixer. Add the boiling water to the chocolate chips. When the chocolate is melted, blend on low speed.

6. As the mixer is blending on slow speed, add the frothy egg replacer, oil, and vanilla. Mix until well combined.

7. Add the dry ingredients to the bowl and continue to mix on slow speed. Scrape the sides of the bowl with a spatula and mix again until slightly lumpy.

8. Add the thickened soy milk and continue to mix at slow speed until the batter is well combined and smooth. Do not overmix.

9. Pour the batter into the prepared pan and bake for 65 to 75 minutes. Rotate the pan halfway through the baking time. Test the cake with a toothpick to determine doneness.

10. Remove the cake from the oven and let sit for 15 minutes. While still warm, invert the pan onto a cake platter, turn, and lift the cake off the pan. Let the cake cool completely before serving, as the moisture needs time to evaporate. Once the cake is completely cool, pour Dark Chocolate Glaze (page 130) over the top and let it drizzle over the sides and form a luscious puddle on the cake plate. Or, for a contrast to the chocolate, the Easy Icing (page 131) goes nicely with this cake as well.

Makes 1 bundt cake; 12 slices

Dark Chocolate Glaze

Satiny, rich glaze to drizzle over cakes and brownies. Keep a bowl
of berries nearby for dunking!

⅓ cup Silk Original Creamer

¼ cup light corn syrup

1 teaspoon vanilla extract

⅔ cup Divvies Semisweet
Chocolate Chips

1. Combine the creamer, corn syrup, and vanilla in a medium saucepan. Bring the mixture to a boil, stirring often.

2. Once it has reached a boil, remove the pan from the heat, add the chocolate chips, and whisk until smooth.

3. Allow the glaze to cool to room temperature. Spoon the glaze over the cooled cake.

Makes 1 cup glaze

Easy Icing

Make this icing once, and you'll see why I call it "Easy"!

1. Beat with a spoon by hand the confectioners' sugar and 3 tablespoons of rice milk, until well combined. If you would like the icing to be thinner and runnier, add more rice milk.
2. If desired, add a tiny drop of food coloring while mixing. Add additional drops of coloring, little by little, until your color choice is achieved.
3. Drizzle the icing over cake or cookies, or spread evenly using the back of a spoon.

Makes 1 cup icing

1 cup confectioners' sugar

3 to 6 tablespoons rice milk or soy milk

Food coloring, in the color of your choice (optional)

Chocolate-Dipped Candy Shop Pretzel Sticks

These look and taste like fancy chocolate-dipped pretzels from a high-end, gourmet candy shop. When served in beautiful glass cups, they also make eye-popping table decorations. I love giving these as party favors. Wrap them in cellophane bags with lots of colorful curling ribbon tied on the top end. I prefer to make these with pretzel rods, but the traditional pretzel twists are equally impressive.

1 cup Divvies Semisweet Chocolate Chips

1/2 teaspoon canola oil

One 10-ounce bag pretzel rods or twists

FOR DECORATIONS (OPTIONAL)

Crushed peppermint hard candies

Crushed cinnamon hard candies

Rainbow sprinkles

Chocolate sprinkles

Themed sprinkles (hearts, snowflakes, etc.)

Colored sugars

1. Line a baking sheet with wax paper.
2. Place the sprinkles or candies, if using, on individual paper plates and set aside.
3. Place the chocolate chips in a wide, shallow microwave-safe bowl. Add the canola oil to the unmelted chips. Melt the chips at medium or high power for 1 1/2 minutes. Remove from the microwave and stir so the melted chips can melt the unmelted ones. If necessary, continue heating in 15-second intervals, stirring in between until all chips are melted and the chocolate is very smooth.
4. Dip each pretzel rod about one-fourth of the way into the chocolate. You may want to use a small spatula or a butter knife to spread the chocolate so it looks smooth.
5. Lay the coated pretzels on wax paper–lined baking sheets, lining up the rods in the same direction. Leave a bit of space between each pretzel.
6. If decorating, allow the chocolate to set for 1 minute, but not completely. Roll each pretzel rod in the desired topping (or just sprinkle them on). Allow to set completely for 30 minutes before serving or wrapping.

Makes 15 to 20 pretzel sticks

Apple Fritters

Hot, fried, sweetened dough with lots of powdered sugar . . . everyone loves this early-summer carnival staple, in the form of a zeppole, pancake, or funnel cake. My version comes out similar to zeppoles (or what I like to call Little Balls of Heaven). Mix up a batch of my quick glaze and drizzle over the fritters for extra deliciousness!

1. Whisk the flour, sugar, and baking powder together in a medium-size bowl.

2. Add the applesauce, vanilla, and water to the flour mixture. Using a large spoon, stir all the ingredients until well combined. The consistency will be similar to bread dough. Set aside.

3. Pour oil into a large saucepan and place on the stove over high heat (350 degrees). The oil should be deep enough to completely cover the fritters while frying, so add more oil if necessary.

4. Scoop ½ teaspoon of batter and use another spoon to push it into the oil. Fry in batches of eight until the fritters float to the top and turn golden brown (about 2 minutes), then flip them to fry the other side. Be careful not to burn the batter.

5. To determine the length of frying time, and to test for doneness, use a sharp knife to cut a ball in half. The dough should be cooked all the way through. Note that the longer the oil remains heating over the stove, the hotter it will become. You may need to reduce the level of heat over the duration of the cooking time.

6. Remove from the saucepan and let the fritters drain on paper towels.

FRITTERS

1¾ cups all-purpose flour

¾ cup white sugar

1 teaspoon baking powder

¼ cup smooth applesauce

½ tablespoon vanilla extract

¾ cups water

4 cups canola oil

½ cup confectioners' sugar

QUICK GLAZE (OPTIONAL)

2 cups confectioners' sugar

1½ tablespoons rice milk

7. While still hot, sprinkle the dough liberally with confectioners' sugar, or drizzle with quick glaze.

8. For the glaze, stir the confectioners' sugar and rice milk together in a medium-size bowl. Drizzle the glaze over fritters. Wait two minutes for glaze to harden, turn fritters over, and repeat. Serve immediately.

Makes 4 dozen 1-inch fritters

Variations: Substitute ¼ cup mashed ripened banana for the applesauce. For an extra-tasty topping, add ½ teaspoon cinnamon to the confectioners' sugar and sprinkle on top.

Benjamin on birthdays!

Mom: What do you love most about birthday parties?

Benjamin: One of the best things you can do as a kid is to get together with friends and just hang out. Birthdays are perfect reasons to get together. I love Piñatas. You never know what's in them. I love when you buy the unfilled ones and then stuff them with unexpected stuff like small toys and gadgets. It's fun when it's not just all candy. But, if I'm at someone's party and end up with candy I'm allergic to, I just trade it for something I can eat.

What's your idea of a great birthday party?

The best party would be a New York Mets baseball party. All my friends would be together. No one would be discussing my food allergies or making comments. We would go to a Mets game and the chefs at the stadium would know how to make the foods that my friends and I love to eat. After the game, we'd have a sleepover in a tent and I'd pass around safe treats—like Divvies. It would be fun because we would all be eating the same food and everyone would be eating food they love.

Have you learned any important lessons about your food allergies over the years?

When I was little, I thought it wasn't fair that I had food allergies and when it came to eating, I didn't like being at birthday parties. Now that I'm older, I can handle attending birthday parties without my parents and communicating about my food allergies and what needs to be done with food in order for me to be safe. I still get frustrated when everyone can eat something I can't have. But I just take a deep breath and break out food you have sent along with me to the party that everyone can enjoy. Bringing something that everyone likes to eat and everyone can share . . . that really makes me feel great.

Make Your Own Party Favors!

The four hand-crafted candy party favors that follow are always a big hit because kids love going home with something special and unique that they've made themselves. Plus, the crafts can be created quickly and simply (the Sandler boys like to work fast!) or quite elaborately. Using allergen-safe candies makes the experience even more joyful and delicious.

Ready!

- *Set up a convenient workspace for the candy project. It is best to use candies that are allergen-free, so that all guests may enjoy the activity.*
- *Divide candies by variety, color, and size.*
- *Place several spoons or scoops in each bowl of candy so that guests do not use their hands when serving themselves. If your artists are very young, consider giving each their own candy to work with instead of sharing.*
- *Have all nonfood materials prepared in advance to make the project easier.*

Set!

- *Everyone must wash their hands.*
- *Show a few examples of the finished creation to provide inspiration.*
- *Explain the steps involved in making the candy craft.*

Go!

- *Encourage guests to use their imaginations, creativity, and taste buds!*
- *Place a name tag on each child's completed masterpiece and keep in a safe spot until the end of the party.*

Squish Kabobs *Makes 15 kabobs*

Have your kids make candy Squish Kabobs to sell at fundraisers. They're so easy to make, inexpensive, and have a long shelf life. Reminder: Most gummy candies contain gelatin, so if you are making vegan treats, you will want to use Surf Sweets nut-free, vegan gummies. See In the Pantry on page 8 for more information.

1 cup Divvies Super Stars
1 cup gummy bears
1 cup Swedish Fish
1 cup gummy frogs
1 cup gummy worms
1 cup gum drops
1 cup gummy fruits
15 skewers (about 10 inches long)

1. Sort candies into separate bowls and lay out fifteen 10-inch wooden skewers.
2. Spear about ten candies on each skewer.
3. Wrap in cellophane and tie with lots of colorful curling ribbon.

Jelly Bean Mosaics

Have you ever seen tile mosaics? Imagine replacing tiles with jelly beans! This is a great project for kids because it's easy, fun, and no matter what, the results will be beautiful. You can order special jelly beans by the individual color from Divvies. Please note: The mosaics are not edible!

Divvies Jelly Beans
Craft glue
Card stock paper or heavier

1. Using a pencil, draw your design directly onto the paper.
2. Trace the design with glue (one section at a time).
3. Apply the desired colored jelly beans directly onto the glue.
4. Allow the glue to dry completely, about 45 minutes, before moving the mosaic.

Jelly Bean "Sand Art"

This is so easy and satisfying for very young children. Plus, it's fun to watch their creative process unfold—"One jelly bean for me, and one jelly bean for the jar; one jelly bean for me . . ." You can order special jelly beans by color from Divvies.

Divvies Jelly Beans

1. Pre-label jars with lids with the name of each party guest.
2. Pour the jelly beans into bowls, dividing them by color.
3. Place small scoops in each bowl—scoops work better than spoons for young children.
4. Have a sample jar or two made up so that the children understand the project.
5. Pour the colored jelly beans into jars in layers, or any way the artists design them. Once filled to the top, tightly cover the jars.

Candy Necklaces *Makes 4 necklaces*

This is really an art project as well as a snack—so get their creative juices going, and feed them at the same time. When making candy necklaces with very young children, who are less dexterous, you may prefer to use only pipe cleaners instead of licorice strings, and only Froot Loops.

Red licorice strings or pipe cleaners
Life Savers
Froot Loops
Gummy Life Savers

1. Separate the candies and/or Froot Loops into bowls, either by style or by color.
2. Provide each child with several licorice strings and/or pipe cleaners, and encourage them to be creative in making their own candy jewelry by stringing the licorice through the candy holes.
3. To create necklaces and bracelets, tie the ends of each licorice string together when the children are finished decorating them.

Resources

Food Allergy Initiative (FAI) **www.faiusa.org.** FAI's goal is to fund research that seeks a cure for food allergies; to improve diagnosis and treatment; and to keep patients safe through education and advocacy.

Food Allergy and Anaphylaxis Network (FAAN) **www.foodallergy.org.** FAAN's mission is to provide advocacy and education, and to advance research on behalf of all those affected by food allergies and anaphylaxis.

Dr. Jules Spotts, Ph.D. **www.julesspotts.com.** Dr. Spotts uniquely approaches working privately and in the school setting with children and adults who have food allergies. He has positively impacted their mental, emotional, and psychological health, so they can go about living their daily lives without letting the fact that they have food allergies "define them," as Benjamin says!

Divvies **www.divvies.com.** Divvies makes fun foods, available to share with families and friends across the country. Divvies cookies, popcorns, cupcakes, and chocolates are made in the company's dedicated facility where no peanuts, tree nuts, eggs, or milk enter the doors. Parts of Divvies Bakery are gluten-free, too.

With Heartfelt Thanks

I am very grateful for the love and support so many incredible people have given to Benjamin, Max, Adam, Mark, Divvies, and me; and for not defining Benjamin or our family by his food allergies. Thank you for keeping Benjamin safe so he can go about the business of being a regular kid. Thank you to all our Divvies customers, especially those who have given our treats as gifts in order to sweeten the lives of others.

Mark Daniel, you are the love of my life. Thank you for Adam, Max, and Benjamin, your unconditional love, understanding, optimism, wisdom, intelligence, perseverance, and humor. Divvies would not exist without you.

Adam, Max, and Benjamin, you are my angels from heaven and I love you with all my heart. You are the inspirations behind Divvies' inclusive philosophy. Thank you for being exactly who each of you are, and for taking care of one another's hearts. Adam and Max, the way you have always protected Benjamin from unsafe foods is awesome. Benjamin, the way you bravely live life to the fullest touches all who know you.

Mommy and Daddy, I love you. I will always know everything you have ever taught me. Thank you for running Divvies' Old Tappan PR Department.

Andrea, you are the one who has unconditionally believed in Divvies from the beginning. I love you for being Divvies' greatest cheerleader and a true-blue friend who can always make me laugh. My sidecar is reserved for you! A special thank-you for sharing your mom's granola recipe.

David and Ann, I will always be grateful to you for getting Benjamin to the hospital so quickly and staying by our side. I love and admire you.

Evan (Bottom Toot) and Mia (my Honey Bunny), you are the icing on my cake! I cherish every second we are together. Love you so much.

Susan, thank you for bringing your beautiful energy to Divvies. You do so much for which I am grateful . . . especially your loyalty and support to Mark.

Audrey, thank you for creating so many special moments for Benjamin, Max, and Adam.

Eric, thank you for caring so much about Divvies and our family.

Dr. Spotts, thank you for your unconditional guidance. You have impacted our family in the most positive way. Divvies' philosophy comes from all you have taught us.

Susan, Hugo, Magdalena, Geide, Marianna, Claudia, Jody, Emily, Susan, Nancy, and the entire Divvies staff, thank you for all of your dedication and hard work. You are what makes the Divvies experience so wonderfully special.

Kim, thank you for showering Divvies with all of your designing creativity, talent, instincts, and wisdom. I am so grateful to you for understanding my vision. Mark and I love and appreciate your friendship most of all.

Richard, I know you know this . . . you are so cool, kind, and talented. Thank you for making Divvies look as good as it does.

Tom, thank you for all of your great designing.

Sandee, thank you for not laughing at my baking methods and for introducing me to the world of professional baking equipment.

Jack, thank you for being my science tutor! I am grateful for your patience during the recipe-creation phase of Divvies.

Lisa, Daphne, Patty Alice, Andrea, and Lorri, thank you for your friendship and working on Divvies' very first assembly line!

All of Benjamin's awesome friends and their families, thank you for keeping an open mind, treating Benjamin just like everyone else, and including him in all the fun while doing your part to keep him safe from the foods he is allergic to.

Matthew, Reece, Nathan, Jack Q., Ryan, Jack Green, Brendan, Sam, James, Sean, Max, and your moms and dads, the kindness you have extended to Benjamin brings tears to my eyes. I cannot thank you enough for all the times you hosted Benjamin on playdates, overnights, and dinners making sure all his food was safe. And thank you for willingly accepting the responsibility of possibly having to use his EpiPen.

Marlene, thank you for keeping Benjamin safe in a most caring manner.

Robin and Joel, Mark and I will be forever grateful to you for bringing Benjamin (he is a "talker"!) to Shea Stadium and doing a superb job of taking care of him so he could have a memory of a lifetime. Robin, thank you for sharing your apple pie recipe. It's Benjamin's favorite!

The Z's, Landoodies, K's, Suzanne, Bernacchias, and Brenners, thank you for always making it possible for Benjamin to feel included and enjoy a delicious, safe meal when we are together. Our collective appreciation of great food in the spirit of friendship has inspired me every step of the way. I love you all!

Andrew, thank you for sharing your marketing and branding expertise . . . and more importantly for your friendship and sense of humor!

Joan and Jerry, thank you for making special latkes at Chanukah and for all the meal planning you have done so Benjamin and Timmy can enjoy their reunions.

NY Jet Tailgating Crew, Drs. Steve, Frank, Ken, and Mitch, thanks for welcoming Benjamin and keeping your grill safe for his hamburgers!

All of my taste testers, I'm afraid to start listing names, as there are so many. Thank you for tasting my concoctions and giving your honest feedback. You have been more helpful than you can possibly imagine.

Lynn and Mary (Trinity Tots), Gary and Barbara Bloom (Playland Nursery School and Camp Playland), Virginia (Canaan Ridge Nursery School), thank you for giving us peace of mind whenever Benjamin attended your schools and camp. You couldn't have done more to make his experience better.

Pound Ridge Elementary School, I wish every school would make the educational experience as inclusive and positive for all students as PRES has. Special thank-yous to Mrs. Schreier, Mrs. Luppino, Mrs. Pearl, Mr. Byrne, Mrs. Kolb, Ms. DeLesia, Mrs. D'Urso, Dr. Sgroi, Mr. Politi, Mrs. Stoeffler, Mrs. Quinn, and Mrs. Clark.

Fox Lane Middle School—East is the Beast!

Camp Wingate Kirkland, thank you Sandy, Will, Janet, and the entire staff. You have made every wish Mark, Benjamin, and I have come true. You have provided Benjamin with his home away from home.

Benjamin's soccer, baseball, basketball, football, and wrestling coaches, thank you for never thinking twice about what needed to be done to provide Benjamin with an inclusive, safe experience. Your positive attitude toward coaching and seeing the big picture is what makes Pound Ridge a fantastic community.

Grace, Frank, Frankie, Bobby, Eduardo, Jesus, Richie, and the gang at Marcella's Pizza in Mount Kisco, New York, thank you for always warmly welcoming Benjamin with the tastiest lunches and dinners. You have gone above and beyond in ensuring Benjamin's happiness and safety!

New England Pediatrics (Drs. Klenk, Levine, Morelli, Palker, and Davis, Diane, Lynn, Chris, Sashni, and Gretchen, thank you for taking care of our entire family both medically and emotionally. You truly understand the psychological implications of food allergies and how they affect families.

The Jaffe Food Allergy Institute at Mount Sinai Hospital, everyone who sees Benjamin: Drs. Sicherer, Sampson, and Nowak; Jessica, Beth, Christian, Gayle, Pearl, Diego, Sally, and Marion. Your fine work touches so many families. We cannot thank you enough for including Benjamin in your egg and milk studies. Your incredible level of expertise, professionalism, and sensitivity supports Benjamin's courage to participate in these magnificent studies. Thanks to you, a world of "new" foods is available to Benjamin and so many.

Celeste Fine, thank you for proposing the idea of creating a Divvies cookbook.

Alyse Diamond, thank you for "getting" Divvies and me right off the bat, and for wanting to publish *The Divvies Bakery Cookbook.* I am grateful for your inclusive style.

Robin Warner, thank you for so kindly sharing your publishing expertise during the auction process.

Tom, Tamara, and Justine, thank you for believing in and giving 100 percent to the photography, set design, and food styling for this book.

Index

Notes from My Kitchen

....

....

....

....

....

....

....

....

....

....

....

....

....

....

Notes from My Kitchen

Notes from My Kitchen